W9-CCB-872

# TREASURES IN YOUR ATTIC

## BOOKS ON COLLECTING
### by Amoret and Christopher Scott

| | |
|---|---|
| *A-Z of Antique Collecting,* | Max Parrish |
| *Collecting Bygones,* | ,, |
| *Tobacco and the Collector,* | ,, |
| *Dummy Board Figures,* | Golden Head |
| *Antiques as an Investment,* | Oldbourne |
| *The Collecting Book,* | Michael Joseph |
| *Discovering Staffordshire Figures,* | Shire Publications |
| *Discovering Smoking Antiques,* | ,, |

### by Amoret Scott and Roy Curtis
| | |
|---|---|
| *Portobello Passport,* | Macdonald |

# TREASURES
# IN YOUR ATTIC

by
Amoret and Christopher Scott

*Illustrated by Jannat Houston, with 20 photographs
by Christopher Scott*

KAYE & WARD
LONDON

First published by Kaye & Ward Ltd
1971

Copyright © 1971 Amoret and Christopher Scott

All Rights Reserved. No part of this publication may be
reproduced, stored in a retrieval system or transmitted, in
any form or by any means, electronic, mechanical, photo-
copying, recording or otherwise, without the prior per-
mission of the Copyright owner.

ISBN 0 7182 0788 2

All enquiries and requests relevant to this title should
be sent to the publisher, Kaye & Ward Ltd, in the City
of London, and not to the printer.

Printed in Great Britain by
Willmer Brothers Limited, Birkenhead

For Gerald Morice

# Contents

# Introduction
# Attics and treasures

The boom in antiques goes on. As people become better off, have better houses to live in and have more time to think and look around them, an increasing number turn to antiques as investments.

The difficulty is that as more people want to collect antiques, supplies become more difficult to find. One doesn't have to be an economist to realize that

(a) no more antiques—genuine ones that is—can be created so

(b) the supply must be spread thinner as more people want to collect, unless

(c) more genuine antiques can be found.

It is the last bit, 'unless more genuine antiques can be found', that this book is all about. There is no doubt that hidden away in the attics of the British Isles there is a vast treasurehouse of the sort of material that collectors are eagerly searching for. And it is not just in the attics of large country houses that these treasures are to be found. Terraced houses in the mining valleys of Wales and Victorian semi-detached properties on the outskirts of industrial towns are just as likely to have the pieces that collectors want.

Dealers have known this for a long time. Every now and again, the 'knockers' will descend on a district. Not all of them are unscrupulous in their methods, but there are enough that are to have put the public on their guard. What usually happens is this. The 'knocker' arrives at your front door and asks if you have any old things to sell. He isn't put off if you say no, and starts listing the things he is looking for—'Any old candlesticks, missus? Bits of china? I'll give you a good

9

price.' Before you quite know how it happened he is inside the house, going quickly round every room, picking things up and looking at them, talking all the time, even going upstairs. His method is to go on and on, badgering away until at last you accept some ridiculous sum for a handsome old chair or a watch that belonged to your great-great-grandfather, simply for the sake of getting rid of him.

This sort of thing happens nearly every day, even in the most remote rural villages. It is very difficult to deal with. If there is a man about the house, then the 'knocker' probably won't take the risk of forcing his way in. But of course he usually chooses a time to call when the man is likely to be out at work, and there is just the wife at home. Even worse are the cases where old people, often living alone, are swindled in this way out of pieces that are not only valuable in terms of money, but have family associations which are even more important to the owner. The only way to get rid of 'knockers' of this kind is to refuse to let them in; and if they do barge their way past, to make a real fuss about it. Call for a neighbour (don't leave the 'knocker' alone in your house whatever you do) and, of course, if you have a telephone, ring up the police. Get the number of his car—it may help. But unless he has actually stolen something, it is very difficult for the police to make a charge stick. So the moral is—don't let him come in.

But they always say prevention is better than cure. If you know what you have in your house, including those bits and pieces tucked away in the attic, and if you have some idea of what is valuable among them, you are far less likely to be taken in by the sort of gentleman we have been talking about. More important (because you may go through life and never have a 'knocker' come to your door) you may find that the contents of your attic is not the heap of old junk you always thought it was. It may represent a nest egg, large or small, and you may have been totally unaware of its existence.

You will probably be astonished, after reading this book, at the things people want to collect and are willing to pay money for. Whatever you think of, there is someone, somewhere in the world, who collects it. But it is quite certain that as long as it remains in your attic, nobody is going to get the chance to see it and to buy it. Read this book, pull the loft ladder down, climb up into the dusty darkness, open up those old trunks and look inside. You may well find quite a lot of the things we talk about in the following pages.

If you do find treasures, what are you going to do about it? It depends very much on what it is you find, and the amount you want to dispose of. *Books* are easy: if you have a reasonable quantity—say a couple of dozen or more—ask the local bookshop owner to call and he will give you a valuation in your own home. If he buys them, the valuation will be free (and there is an unwritten rule, by the way, that you don't ask another book dealer for a competitive valuation). *Stamps,* including envelopes with the stamps still on them, are equally straightforward; if there is no stamp dealer in your local town, there are plenty in London, and you can post off your treasures to them and ask them for a valuation with perfect confidence. If you have large pieces of *furniture* in your attic, you should ask the local antique dealer to call. He may make a charge for this—you should find out first.

Anything which does not fit easily into the 'antique' category (such as clothes, toys, old souvenirs, albums and so on) are more difficult to deal with. There are some dealers who specialize in unexpected things, and where possible we have mentioned names and addresses in the appropriate section of this book. There are also a surprisingly large number of clubs which not only have meetings but correspond among their members about specialist interests; again, these are mentioned where appropriate. In cases of real doubt, probably the best answer is to take the object to your local museum. In nine cases out of ten the curator or his assistants will be able to tell you what the thing is and when it was made, and who might want to buy it—sometimes a local collector, more often a local dealer. When you are certain of what you want to sell, and have at least a rough idea of what you expect to get for it, an advertisement in the antiques or books section of the weekly *Exchange and Mart* may well do the trick. Take it for a few weeks first (or see it at the library) to give you an idea of what gets advertised; and when you put in your own, have a box number rather than making your own address public—just in case.

11

We would *not* advise you to put things into the local sale-room. Every small town has one, sometimes two or three. They usually hold a weekly auction sale where anything from old television sets to mousetraps is disposed of to the highest bidder. The trouble is that such sale-rooms, although they do an excellent job as middlemen between the general selling public and the general buying public, very rarely have any specialized knowledge. The result is that anything they are not sure about tends to get lumped with other miscellaneous items into one lot, which might well be sold for a fraction of its true value. It is true that most of the local antique dealers or their representatives go to these sales, and now and again you will get a good price for an antique or a bygone because the dealers compete for it. But on the whole it is a very risky way of disposing of anything which could conceivably have a value. Even worse is to answer one of those advertisements in the local paper—'Houses cleared. Everything taken'—because the advertisers rely on quick turnover of cheap stuff. Anything doubtful gets burned, or at best passed over to the local sale-room in a miscellaneous lot.

Having built up your hopes of finding treasures worth thousands of pounds in your attic, we must now bring you back to earth. There will be a lot of disappointments. We have spent several afternoons standing by the inquiry desk at Sotheby's, the world-famous London auction rooms, watching the stream of people who bring things along to be put into one of the sales. Almost invariably they think they have brought a treasure. Three times out of four they have to be told that the object has virtually no value, because it is not what they thought it was, or because it is a modern copy, or because it is a fake. We have watched people bring in 'Stradivarius' violins made by a jobbing carpenter in 1920; an 'original' letter from Queen Victoria that was an obvious facsimile (see Chapter 1); and so on. Not every ugly duckling is a swan.

The other note of warning to be sounded is about condition. A rare Victorian Staffordshire pottery figure (see Chapter 9) may be worth more than £100. But if one arm is missing, or even if the arm has been knocked off and joined on again, that same figure will probably be worth less than

£10, or perhaps even nothing. The same rule applies to almost everything else which is collectable—postcards that are 'foxed' (that is, covered with brown marks); books with even one page missing; teapots without their lids; or coins where the design is worn a little flat through use.

You will find, in later chapters of this book, occasional references to fakes and forgeries and reproductions. As a rule, this is much more of a problem to the collector who is buying from a shop or through an advertisement. There are not likely to be many 'wrong 'uns' in the attic, simply because the contents of the attic have, for the most part, been there for quite a long time.

Don't build up your hopes too high. Nevertheless, the likelihood is that in *your* house there are things that you have no further use for and which collectors want to buy. And who knows, there really might be a treasure in your attic.

Finally, it is worth remembering that treasures are not always expressed in terms of hard cash. A rare butterfly, or a photograph of a steam plough in action, may be worth little in sale value; but to an impecunious collector it might be the thing he has searched for all his life.

# I

# Paper

The amount of paper that man produces every day is frightening. Think of newspapers, magazines, books, wrapping paper, wallpaper, cartons, writing paper, cardboard, handkerchiefs—even furniture and clothes these days. Most of this mountain of paper becomes rubbish as soon as it has done the job it was designed for. But like so many other things, certain kinds of paper which have been put away for a number of years acquire a scarcity value, and are therefore collected. Attics, by their very nature as places where things are put away because they are no longer wanted, can be a rich source of this collectable paper.

**Postcards** The centenary of the first British postcard was in 1970 (Austria beat us by a whisker in bringing out the very first postcard in 1869). Books about early postcards were published last year, and there were big exhibitions in London and elsewhere. This has given a boost to postcard collecting. But there is another important reason why postcards are likely to be increasingly collected. Until 1968 it was cheaper to send a postcard through the post than it was to send a letter. Now they cost the same, and you pay extra simply for getting your communication (letter or postcard) there a bit faster. The natural result is that the postcard is getting less popular every year. Since the postal charges have recently gone to 3p for first-class mail and $2\frac{1}{2}$p for second-class the days of the postcard as a means of communication have almost come to an end. So now is as good a time as ever to look out those old postcard albums.

Until the last war, everybody sent postcards to everybody else. If you have not seen a well-filled Victorian or Edwardian postcard album, you can scarcely imagine the variety—not just views (although there were of course a great many) but wonderful novelty ones, naughty ones, commemorative ones and so on. Even extraordinarily dull-looking examples can be very exciting to specialist collectors. Here are some which are particularly sought after:

*Hand-embroidered silk postcard – First World War*

*War* There were a good many minor wars in Africa during the last quarter of the nineteenth century, culminating in the Boer War of 1899–1902. Postcards of generals, battles won, sieges lifted, medals awarded—all these are collectors' items. Between the end of the Boer War and the beginning of the Great War there was a period of uneasy peace. The Great War produced a tremendous volume of postcards, and there are now many collectors who specialize in this narrow field. Particularly collected are the postcards embroidered in silk with bright colours, nearly all of them made in France (a few in Belgium). Despite each one having been made individually by hand, they were turned out in thousands, if not millions. The subjects include flags of the allies, patriotic slogans, family greetings, simple pictures of flowers and seasonable messages. Some have the date incorporated into the embroidered design. Best of all are the embroidered regimental badges and the inserted photographs of French and British generals. The more common kind of embroidered silk fetches up to 40p each; regimental badges up to £1.25. Many of them are made in the form of an envelope of material, inside which there should be a little card printed in colour, usually with a message such as 'Greetings from France'.

Bruce Bairnsfather, who created the immortal character Old Bill, designed a large number of postcards. There are specialist collectors of Bairnsfather material, and a complete set of Bairnsfather First World War cards (including such classics as 'Well, if you knows of a better 'ole, go to it'; 'Coiffure in the trenches'; 'At present we are staying at a farm'; and 'Gott strafe this barbed wire') will find a ready market.

There is a very long set (well over a hundred) of cards photographically produced by the *Daily Mail* showing scenes in all theatres of the war. This is quite common, and of no great value unless the complete set is all together. But *foreign* postcards of the First World War, particularly any from the enemy nations, are eagerly collected. So are naval and flying cards of the period—there are many collectors who specialize in First World War flying material.

The British, with their notorious sense of humour, were able to find a good deal of fun in the Great War, in spite of Passchendaele and the Somme. A large number of amusing postcards based on war episodes and subjects were produced, including such things as elderly spinsters looking dolefully at posters saying 'Kitchener gets 500,000 men' and regretting that they could not even get one. There are also mock German cards showing fat and terrified Prussian soldiers shouting 'Look out, der Royal Field Artillery [or the 6th Dragoon Guards or the Royal Inniskilling Fusiliers as the case might be] are koming!' Also collected are the bare and poignant Field Service postcards which soldiers at the Front could send back in the brief moments to spare between attacks;

he merely had to select a few phrases from a number of printed alternatives such as 'I am well/I have been wounded /Your letter received/I have not heard from you for *x* months'. For all their brevity, some of these brief brown postcards are very sad. Many of the senders were killed the same day.

Postcards showing pictures of tanks, or submarines, or ambulances, or searchlights, are all wanted by specialist collectors. Some subjects are of course rarer than others; references to the Royal Naval Air Service or Bicycle Battalions are valued more highly than commoner subjects.

There was a large range of highly sentimental and sometimes religious cards from the Great War. They deal with mothers thinking of their sons away at war, sons away at war thinking of their mothers and girlfriends at home, and all looking forward to the day when they will be reunited. There is nearly always a verse as well as a picture on the postcards, and most of them are typical of the worst form of sentimentality. They will almost certainly be collected for their horror value, but at the moment they are priced at the low end of the scale.

Individual postcards of the First World War, disregarding special rarities, are worth between 2½p and 12p. This does not sound much, but postcard albums frequently hold as many as two hundred individual cards.

*See-throughs or Hold-to-lights* These were made in various forms. The most usual is an evening scene with houses, and perhaps a ship on the sea or a lighthouse on the coast; when you hold it to the light the windows of the houses or the portholes of the ship are translucent and the whole scene looks as if it is a picture at night. They are very attractive.

*Named artists* Some of the artists who specialized in making drawings for postcards are now collected in their own right. Among them are Louis Wain, famous for his pictures of cats. He did a lot of postcards, all of them signed on the front. Sadly, he gradually lost his mind and the development of his madness can clearly be seen in the sort of cats he drew. In his early days, they were soft and cuddly and attractive, but towards the end of his life they are huge and bristling with mad staring eyes.

Another artist who is now being collected is Donald McGill, who was responsible for most of the naughty seaside postcards involving huge women and little men in embarrassing situations. Like Louis Wain, he also signed all his cards.

*Novelties* Ever anxious to find something different, the Victorian and Edwardian postcard designers turned out mechanical cards (for example, you pull a string and a man's arm spanks a pretty girl), cards printed on peat or leather, cards with moving eyes or tails, cards with real hair or real clothes, and so on. An interesting sidelight on these novelties is that the postal authorities charged extra for carrying any card that was more than a plain cardboard. Even the ones decorated with a sprinkling of silver tinsel were surcharged, because they caught the postman's fingernails!

*General* We obviously cannot deal with every type and subject-matter of postcards, for the range is colossal. But among the types which are particularly collected are advertising cards (either for events or for products); political ones including such things as the suffragette movement; royalty; early transport (trams, horse buses, railway engines); early seaside, particularly showing bathing machines; actors and music-hall artists; and of course any postcard of really early date—the nearer to 1870, the more valuable. The postmark will show (if it has been through the post, of course).

For further information on postcards, refer to *Discovering Picture Postcards* by C. W. Hill, Shire Publications, 1970 (excellent value at 25p); *The Picture Postcard and its Origins* by Frank Staff, Lutterworth Press, 1966; and the recently published *Collecting British Picture Postcards: 1870–1918* by Tonie and Valmai Holt. There is also the Postcard Club of Great Britain (Sec.: Mrs D. Brennan, 34 St James's Crescent, London S.W.9) which issues a bi-monthly newsletter.

**Old newspapers** Newspapers, by their very nature, are intended to be immediately replaceable. Today's newspaper is nearly always completely out of date by tomorrow, and so it gets thrown away or burnt. In 999 cases out of every 1,000 (and that covers only about three years of a daily newspaper) there is no reason why a particular issue should have been preserved. But just occasionally there is. The occasion is nearly always some far-reaching historical event; examples that spring to mind are the assassination of the Archduke Francis Ferdinand at Sarajevo in 1914, which precipitated the First World War; the torpedoing of the *Lusitania* which brought America into the same war; the disaster of the *Titanic* when it struck an iceberg on its maiden voyage in 1912 and sank with appalling loss of life; declarations of war from the Crimean in 1854 onwards; royal deaths and funerals, and so on. Occasionally newspapers containing reports of events of this kind will have been carefully preserved by our grandfathers and put away for the historical documents they are. If they are found in the attic, treat them gently when you unfold them, for old newspaper is extremely brittle. It is difficult to put a value upon material of this kind because as a rule the value is what a collector is prepared to pay you. It is therefore a question of finding the collector, and very often the best way to achieve this is a visit to the curator of your local museum. One word of caution—reprints of very special early newspapers (for example, the issue of the London *Times* containing Nelson's despatch from Trafalgar) have been made, even in Victorian times. They are usually recognizable by having been printed on much better quality paper than would normally have been used.

**Old magazines** Magazines differ from newspapers in several ways. To start with, they were printed on heavier paper and were designed to last longer than the transient newspaper. Secondly, most of them were meant to appeal to a specialist, whether that specialist were a teenage girl interested in soppy love-stories or a collector of Chinese snuff bottles. As a rule the old magazines that are now saleable fall into the following categories:

1. Individual issues covering specific events such as royal funerals.

2. Unbroken runs of specialist or prestige magazines, including those still in production. For example, unbroken runs of such current publications as *Apollo,* the *Burlington Magazine* and *Country Life* are readily saleable: but they *must* be complete (that is, no pages missing from the individual magazines and no issues missing from the run) and ideally they should cover several years, particularly in the case of magazines issued monthly or at less frequent intervals. Also wanted are long complete runs of certain technical prestige magazines such as the *Journal of the Royal United Services Institution* and the *Journal of the Royal Horticultural Society.* The best way of selling such runs of current publications is to advertise in the magazine itself.

3. Defunct magazines. Many well-known magazines with long and honourable histories have succumbed to economic pressures, particularly since the end of the last war. Among them are *Picture Post* and *John Bull.*

4. Famous names. Magazines containing the work, particularly the early work, of figures who later became famous are much collected. The early writings and illustrations of Winston Churchill are an example. If there are doubts about an author or illustrator, the *Dictionary of National Biography* at your local public library will tell you if the name is a really well-known one, and may also provide evidence about dates. For example, it will tell you when the first Sherlock Holmes story by Sir Arthur Conan Doyle appeared in the *Strand* magazine; and if you have that issue it's a collectors' gem.

**Albums**   The Victorians had an absolute passion for filling scrap albums. It was mainly a female hobby and it occupied the long winter evenings at a time when there was no radio to listen to and no television to look at. Mothers and daughters took pride in filling their scrap books, arranging them artistically and comparing them with those of their friends. There is no doubt that, sadly, a great many of these Victorian scrap albums have been thrown away or burnt as large houses have been converted into flats and demolished to make way for new development. However, for every one that appears for sale, there are certainly fifty hidden away. Collectors are very keen on them, and they are well worth looking out.

Among the things that young ladies stuck with loving care into their scrap albums were Christmas cards and Valentines (early examples of both can be very valuable), advertisements, cigar labels, bottle labels and the colourful scraps which were bought in sheets specially for embellishing albums.

Albums of old *photographs* are on the whole quite worthless unless they show people or events of importance.

*Victorian scrapbook*

**Books**  It is unlikely that you are going to come across a very valuable book in the attic. The whereabouts of the really early writings—contemporary editions of Chaucer and the like—are known to the nearest square inch. But there is nevertheless a great deal of material under the loose heading of 'books' which is sought by collectors. This material is increasing in volume all the time as collectors turn their attention to new (more recent, in fact) subdivisions. It includes:

*First editions*  A good deal of nonsense is talked about first editions. All books have first editions; most of them never have any more. The trashiest western or teenage romance is published as a first edition, but as it is very unlikely to be reprinted it remains as a single edition which is soon forgotten. But the first printed edition of Shakespeare's plays, known as the First Folio, was published in 1623 and is almost priceless; it has been followed by countless thousands of printings in almost every language in the world.

In between these two extremes there are first editions which could well be found hidden away in an attic—first editions of Jane Austen or Dickens, George Bernard Shaw or Hilaire Belloc, of Disraeli or Winston Churchill. The business of knowing about books is a highly expert and professional one, and no amateur can learn enough about it to be really sure. If you discover old books written by well-known authors you can at least find out whether it is worth pursuing any further by finding a biography of that author in the public library. This will tell you when his or her works were first published, and you will therefore know whether your book could be a first edition or not. Very often the month is as important as the year in establishing this. In any case you must accept the word of the bookseller to whom you take them for valuation and (if you wish) sale. They are among the most honest of men.

*Illustrations*   The illustrations of a book can sometimes be more important than the book or its subject matter. For example, Tenniel's illustrations for the original edition of *Alice in Wonderland* and *Through the Looking-Glass* have never been surpassed: when we think of Alice we think of Tenniel's pretty, serious-faced, long-haired little girl. Illustrations by well-known artists will be easily identifiable, not only by the signature on the illustrations themselves, but also in the credits of the book at the beginning. If you discover a book illustrated by an artist who *later* became famous, you will have a real find; again, a very little research in the library will tell you whether you hold a gold nugget or—as the Americans say—a lead balloon.

By the way, if in your attic you come across a book with uncut pages (that is, with some of the pages still joined together at the outer edge) you should on no account cut them.

*Decorated covers*   There is an increasing demand for the extremely attractive decorated book covers of the second half of the nineteenth century. They are usually impressed and gilded (other colours were sometimes used as well, but these tend to be later examples). Of particular interest to collectors —and not necessarily book collectors alone—are the little mid-Victorian embossed-cover books on such subjects as the Language of Flowers, Etiquette for Ladies and Gentlemen, early scientific inventions and, particularly, children's books. These volumes are usually dated in roman figures on the title page.

*Authors' manuscripts* Very few authors' descendants can be unaware of the modern interest in collecting original manuscripts of published works by celebrated literary figures. American universities in particular are snapping these up whenever they appear, and the prices they are prepared to pay are staggering. Any such manuscripts (typescripts corrected in the author's hand, or entirely in longhand) should be treated as a valuable security.

*Private presses* In the middle of the nineteenth century a new movement was founded to revive fine book printing, which had fallen into a decline. The design, printing and binding of the books produced by the private presses are outstanding, and each product is a collectors' piece. Names to look for are Kelmscott Press (founded by William Morris), Doves Press, Ashendene, Golden Cockerel Press and Nonesuch Press. For further reading on the subject of the private presses, and for an excellent introduction to books and book-collecting in general, *Fine Books* by Alan G. Thomas (Pleasures and Treasures series, Weidenfeld & Nicolson, 1967) is recommended.

*Facsimiles* This section is a warning against being misled by facsimiles. The word facsimile comes from the Latin and means, in essence, a copy. It was a method of producing accurate copies of single sheets (which of course could then be bound together into book form), a job which is now done by photocopiers or Xerox machines. Many people have been deceived by facsimiles. We have been shown a book containing facsimiles of such documents as Wellington's despatch from Waterloo, the Declaration of Independence and other priceless historical writings. The owner thought that these were the originals, and that he was about to retire in luxury for the rest of his life. Facsimiles are really quite easy to spot, and they were never made with any intention of deceiving. They are flat in appearance, always in black and white; the blacks are very black. They are nearly always reproduced on a particular kind of commercial paper—as we have said, they are very like modern photocopies. Where a number of individual items have been bound together as a book, or one long facsimile document is divided into pages and bound in this way, there will invariably be a very clear indication somewhere near the title page that this is a facsimile reproduction and not an original.

**Wallpaper** As every home decorator knows, it is always a good idea, when you have finished wallpapering a room, to put the spare rolls away so that if you ever want to do any patching you have the material for it: the manufacturers have a maddening habit of discontinuing patterns after a year or two, so that you can never buy any more. This is not a new thing, and it is very likely that our ancestors had just the same trouble, and took just the same precautions with the beautiful hand-blocked eighteenth-century wallpapers.

Chinese handpainted wallpaper, which was brought into this country at about the middle of the seventeenth century, is probably the most collected. Even earlier papers have been found, however, laboriously printed by hand using a repetition pattern carved on a wooden block and the colours stencilled in afterwards.

It is of course very unlikely that papers of this age will be discovered anywhere other than sticking to walls of houses of the right period. However, during the late nineteenth century there was a great revival in design, and such famous figures as William Morris were responsible for textiles and wallpapers.

Wallpaper collectors (there are a surprising number of them, particularly in America) usually find their most interesting material still attached to walls, often under many more recent layers of wallpaper.

**Typewriters** These come into this chapter because of their association with paper. Industrial archaeology (which concerns itself with the recording and preservation of the way things were made and the machines that made them) has had a very considerable upsurge in the last ten years. Among the off-shoots of the subject are the preservation and collection of domestic machines, including typewriters. The first patented typewriter was produced in the United States in 1829; it was called the Typographer, and a replica of it can be seen in the Science Museum in London. There was very little to connect it, in appearance or operation, with a modern machine. But in 1872 the forerunner of the modern type-writer was produced. It was called the Sholes and Glidden Type-writer, and apart from being much larger and much more ornate than our modern machines, it was surprisingly similar in its method of construction. In collecting terms, 1872 is not very long ago and there could well be some interesting old typewriters tucked away in attics. Names to look out for on such machines are Yost, Swift, Williams, Sun, Postal, Maskelyne, Keystone, Jewett, Lambert and Blick.

# 2

# The post

Like bronchitis, letter-writing could almost be called 'the English disease'. For generations the menfolk have been going off to far-flung bits of the world; during most of the nineteenth century they were acquiring, subduing or defending pieces of the Empire ranging from the edge of the Pacific to the middle of Africa. They wrote their experiences and their thoughts to their relatives at home. Every now and again a war broke out to provide exciting news: Napoleonic from 1803 to 1815, Crimean from 1854 to 1856, Boer from 1899 to 1902, the two Great Wars of the present century, and a whole host of minor wars and skirmishes, most of them in Africa, during the last twenty-five years of Queen Victoria's reign.

Not only have we always been great letter-writers, but at the same time we have always been great hoarders. Missionaries active in the Congo could be almost certain that their descriptions of the pygmies' poisoned darts whistling round their ears would be lovingly preserved by their womenfolk at home. Every soldier away at war would be pretty sure that his brief snatches of news from 'somewhere in France' would be bundled up until he came home.

The trouble was that when he did come home these precious mementoes were often destroyed—they were a sort of insurance policy for his safe return. But there are certainly hoards of letters still bound up in blue or pink ribbon, and with source addresses like Rawalpindi, Mount Everest, Niagara Falls, South Pole, or even just 'On active service', in drawers and boxes and in attics. And among them is a great deal of material that collectors want and will pay handsomely for.

**Autograph letters** Original letters—known as autograph letters—from famous people are valuable. For example, a letter from Sir Winston Churchill written from South Africa when he was a young subaltern during the Boer War would be competed for by collectors all over the world, and would probably go to America at a fat price. Letters from authors, politicians, soldiers and sailors, royalty, murderers—all these are valuable and highly saleable to specialized collectors provided that the writer is a household name. Letters from Private Scroggins will not make you rich—unless of course Private Scroggins happened to be present at the Relief of Ladysmith, or had won a Victoria Cross.

It is by no means only dead personalities whose autographed letters are collected. There is a growing tendency, fostered by American universities, to collect original material about and by living authors. We have already mentioned original manuscripts. In the long run you are almost as likely to get as large a financial return from a letter written by Lawrence Durrell as from one by George Bernard Shaw. Some people think this is an unfortunate development, and it certainly leads to some rather undesirable trading. But it is well worthwhile looking through any bundles of old correspondence, particularly if you happen to know that your family is connected (either by relationship or friendship) with a famous figure. If you find such correspondence, and the figure concerned is *really* famous, it would be worth consulting one of the big London salerooms such as Christie's or Sotheby's. If the person is still alive, it would be polite, at least, to wait until he isn't; alternatively you should write and ask him (or her) whether there is any objection to the correspondence being offered for sale.

**Stamps** Any author who tries to cover the subject of stamp collecting in one subsection of one chapter in a book called *Treasures in your Attic* is playing with fire. However, it must be done. Stamps are among the things most likely to be found on old correspondence, and there is no doubt that there are real treasures to be found in this field, still hidden in hundreds of attics throughout the British Isles. Because of the enormous scope of the subject, we will limit ourselves to a few words of general information and advice.

Early English stamps are among the most valuable of all. There are individual stamps from abroad (usually British colonies) that fetch astronomic prices because only one or two of them are known to exist; but as a general rule English stamps fetch a better price than any others.

If you do find old letters with old stamps on them, treat them like babies. Don't touch the stamps with your fingers, don't try to pick the stamp off the envelope, and above all don't steam or float the stamp away from its envelope. With early and rare stamps the evidence that it has actually been through the post, with perhaps a legible postmark giving an exact date, often represents a difference in value between the commonplace and the desirable. Stamp dealers are extremely fussy about condition. A dirty fingermark on a rare stamp may reduce its value to almost nothing. A stamp dealer always handles his wares with tweezers, never with his fingers.

If you want to do your own investigations into the state and possible value of any old stamps you might find in this way, there are Stanley Gibbons catalogues for the purpose. Values for each stamp are given in these excellent catalogues but it must be remembered always that the values quoted apply only to stamps in perfect condition. There are so many things that can be wrong with an individual stamp—a heavy postmark, a corner torn, dirt and so on. Many people are disappointed when they take old stamps that they have found to a dealer, expecting the full price quoted in the catalogue. Be prepared to have your highest hopes justifiably cut down to size. The best way to find out whether you have a fortune or not is to wrap the envelopes up (with the letters inside as further evidence as to date) and take them to a reputable stamp dealer—not the gentleman on the corner who has one or two packets of stamps hanging in the window: stamp dealing is a highly complex business, and you must put yourself in the hands of the experts.

It may happen that instead of finding individual letters in stamped envelopes, or bundles of such envelopes, you discover old stamp collections complete in their albums. This could be a very exciting find—or once again it could be almost worthless. As in the case of other antiques, there is a general rise in price merely through the passage of time, and consequently a stamp collection gathered together by a father or grandfather is likely to have gone up in value quite considerably. But of course boys—or at least most boys—collect stamps without any idea of realizing the capital value of them at a later date, and as a result many stamp collections are a hotch-potch of valuable and commonplace issues with the accent on eye-appeal. We also remember with a shudder how we used to treat our own stamps: we soaked them off the envelopes in water, mounted them in the albums with dirty, sticky fingers on well-licked hinges, all together so that opposite pages filled with stamps got entangled with each other. You can scarcely blame a stamp dealer (who, after all, is in business to make a profit) for being unenthusiastic about this sort of collection. However, if any of the albums you find were printed for specific or restricted classes of stamp (for example, British issues 1870 to 1900) the chances are that the person who made the collection was serious about it and knew what he was doing. This in turn means, at the least, that the stamps themselves are likely to have been kept in good condition and properly mounted. Take the albums along, complete as they are, to your stamp dealer and ask him for a valuation. He will have a quick look through and if it is anything more than run-of-the-mill material he will probably ask to keep it for a few days so that he can have a careful look through.

Don't forget that there are other things beside ordinary adhesive postage stamps which interest postal collectors. There are postmarks, postage-due stamps, and—often most interesting of all—frankings for the days before adhesive postage stamps were introduced.

Anybody who finds what looks like a really comprehensive and expertly collated stamp collection would be well advised to get in touch with Stanley Gibbons Ltd whose address will be found in the London  telephone directory. They are uniquely qualified to give the right sort of advice in cases like this.

An offshoot of stamp collecting that has become a special subject in its own right is the collection of *first-day covers*.

The term is used to describe the envelope, with its stamp attached, sent through the post on the first day of some particular postal service such as the first airmail flight between two countries, or (more often, these days) the first issue of a new set of stamps. The Post Office Philatelic Bureau in Edinburgh does big business nowadays in producing specially-printed first-day covers for every one of the frequent issues of new stamps. All these will become collectors' items in due course.

*Pictorial writing paper*

**Writing paper** It will probably come as a surprise to many people that writing paper is of interest to collectors. There are in fact two main classes of writing paper which come into this category: pictorial paper, and 'association' paper (by which is meant paper associated with particular places or events).

Pictorial paper is mainly the product of the middle of the nineteenth century. Any town, village or organization that had something to offer the Victorian tourist—scenery, spa water or somebody's birthplace—advertised the facts by putting on sale writing paper headed with charming engravings (see Chapter 8) of the particular attractions. Some of them are most delightful works of art in miniature and are much sought after by collectors—and not only collectors of writing paper but also collectors of any material to do with that particular resort. Earlier letter-writers were accustomed to use a double sheet of paper folded vertically in the middle. With pictorial paper of this period, it is quite common for the whole of the front sheet (page one, as it might be) to be taken up with the pictorial engraving. Later, when single sheets of writing paper became general, most of the top half of the sheet was pictorial. As the century progressed, the little illustrations became smaller until they occupied a small corner of the sheet. Mint (that is, unused) examples of early pictorial writing paper fetches up to 50p a sheet.

'Association' paper is less easy to describe. It is really a question of being aware of the course of history in the last hundred years or so, and keeping a sharp eye open. If, among a bundle of letters you find in your attic, you come across one written on paper headed 'RMS *Titanic*', a small buzzer should sound at the back of your head. If you see that the letter is dated 10 April 1912 (which was the day that the *Titanic* sailed on her maiden voyage, to strike an iceberg a few days later and sink with almost total loss of life) the buzz in your brain should become very loud. There has to be a close correlation between event and date for such 'association' writing paper to be interesting to collectors, but if the association is there, the interest will be great.

**Bills** It would be nice to think that bills, which plague all our lives, could actually be valuable in themselves, and to some extent (though admittedly only a pretty limited one) this can be true. As an example, at Nostell Priory in Yorkshire there are on display some of the original accounts which Thomas Chippendale submitted for furniture which he made for this great house. You can see the actual pieces of furniture side by side with Chippendale's accounts for making them. Such bills are of great historic interest and value, and in consequence they are worth a considerable amount of money.

Very few people are going to come across any original accounts from Chippendale, of course. But there are many

31

fields in which original bills for goods supplied can be valuable, both historically and in terms of money. We know of a small country house that has two paintings of animals by George Stubbs. It is more than likely that somewhere in the house, quite possibly in a trunk in the attic, is the original bill from this best-known of the eighteenth-century animal painters.

The other bills that are of interest to collectors are the much more common eighteenth- and nineteenth-century tradesmen's accounts. These are interesting from two points of view: many of them are illustrated with small engravings (not unlike the pictorial writing paper already mentioned) showing the goods in which the tradesmen dealt; and the goods supplied and the prices paid, in relation to the date of the bill, are often extremely valuable evidence to historians. There was, for example, a recent exhibition, on the subject of Death and Mourning, held at the Royal Pavilion, Brighton; among the items exhibited were undertakers' accounts which showed not only what relatives had to pay for a funeral, but also how incredibly elaborate some of those funerals were. Details such as this play an important part in the piecing together of social history, and although the source material may not be intrinsically valuable, one should be aware of these unexpected treasures in one's attic.

**Christmas cards and Valentines** Several charity organizations appeal every year for you to send them your Christmas cards after you have finished with them. These are sent to some of the underdeveloped countries, where many of the subjects shown are ideal for elementary instruction in the schools: treasures for them, if not for you.

Collectors are on the look-out for early Christmas cards, and rare examples will fetch high prices. The first Christmas card proper was put on sale in 1840. It was slightly smaller than the postcard, and showed a large Victorian family party gathered round a table. On each side were smaller panels showing Charity, feeding and clothing the poor. One thousand of these were lithographed and coloured by hand. It was obvious that this venture was not very successful, because the next commercially produced Christmas card did not appear until 1863. In that year a whole series of cards, quite different in size and style from the 1840 original, was put on sale. They were about the size and shape of a visiting card, with a lacy or embossed border, and a greeting (often surrounded by a bouquet of flowers or a wreath) printed in the middle. This type of card, which at first sold for a penny, rapidly became very popular, and the Christmas card never looked back. Size gradually increased through the years, which (within limits) gives one a good indication of date when one finds a collection of old cards. Christmas cards and Valentines were often mounted in albums—though this has both advantages and disadvantages. They were easier to see, but the method of mounting often makes them almost valueless: as a rule they were firmly stuck in with flour-and-water paste.

Another handsome and much collected type of early Christmas card is the single sheet, heavily decorated with paper lace, often surrounding little vignettes carrying seasonal scenes or greetings. One or two well-known artists produced designs for Christmas cards, among them Kate Greenaway. Devotees of her work are always on the look-out for cards attributable to her.

*Valentine,* circa *1880*

Valentines have a much longer history. By the time the first printed Christmas card appeared, the Valentine was already at the peak of its production; indeed, it was probably on the way down. There are some most delightful examples, both printed and hand-made, among the collections that have been built up on both sides of the Atlantic. The range is so wide and the subject itself so fascinating that it would be wrong to make more than a passing reference to it in a book of this kind. Anyone who finds a bundle of Valentines (and, of all things that a young lady might have kept, Valentines are the most likely) should consult *The Valentine and its Origins* by Frank Staff (Lutterworth Press, 1969).

*Letter balance*

Two other postal items could easily have found their way into the attic. Victorian *letter balances* and *letter scales* are usually identifiable by the nostalgic scales of charges engraved somewhere upon them—'1 oz. for 1d. Each additional oz. $\frac{1}{2}$d.' for example. Balances are usually made of brass and consist of two trays balanced like a see-saw with a pointer between, and a set of round brass weights ranging from $\frac{1}{2}$ oz. to 8 oz. These are just beginning to be collected. Less familiar are the counterweighted balances, usually made of wrought iron and a good deal more complicated in structure. When a letter is put into the tray on top, the counterweighted scales move out sideways like a pair of wings, the point where they finally come to rest showing the weight of the letter.

Finally, there is a steady market for that delightful piece of Victorian furniture, the *posting box*. These were usually found in hotels, country houses and other large establishments, and were intended for the household's (or the guests') letters so that at the times marked the second footman could empty the box of the accumulated letters and take them to post in the nearest GPO public box. They are often wonderful examples of Victorian Gothic, handsomely and solidly made in varnished wood, or sometimes in the form of a real scarlet letterbox. They are typical of the kind of furniture

*Post box from Edwardian country house*

which appeals to modern interior decorators. This is not actually a fate we should recommend for any handsome old posting box, for interior decorators have an unpleasant habit of ruining such pieces by cutting holes in them, or painting them violet or something of the kind; the best thing to use them for is exactly what they were originally designed to do —hold the letters for posting. Many people are looking for them for exactly that purpose, and shops such as 'Trad' and 'Dodo' in London specialize in such things.

# 3
# Children

The delightful thing about children, as many weary mothers must have said, is that they grow up. What happens to all their toys and games, and to their clothes, when they do grow up? It depends to a large extent on how many younger brothers and sisters there are. We all know what happens to children's clothes when there are several in the family: they get passed from number one to number two, from two to three, from three to four, and then they fall to bits.

We will talk more about clothes in Chapter 6, but much the same thing happens, given the same circumstances, to games and toys. But fashions in toys change remarkably quickly. Quite often the toys of five years ago are beneath the dignity of the latest arrival. In this case they are sometimes given away to other less fortunate children, and sometimes they are thrown away; but quite often they are sent up to the attic.

Not long ago we had the good luck of being allowed to take away anything we wanted from a house where a widowed mother had just died. She had never thrown anything away, and the whole house (one of a terrace in the back streets of an industrial town) was a sort of super-attic, where everything was lovingly wrapped and put away in case it might ever be needed again. Among the treasures we found were all her children's (now middle-aged men and women) toys, mostly in their original boxes and wrappings. Even to us who spend our lives looking at this sort of thing, it was a revelation to see the toys and games of the twenties and the thirties, the fashion of the dolls' clothes, the subjects of the jigsaws, the un-

36

abashed little black sambo babies with celluloid heads, the way things were still made to last, and above all the lack of plastics. There were some gems too—collectors' gems, that is; some of them are mentioned in the following pages.

**Games** Of particular interest to collectors are the educational games of the Victorian era. And before we smile too indulgently at the idea, let us not forget that there are one or two card games which have been recently issued to help our own poor brains to understand decimal currency. These will of course be collectors' items in future years, when everyone will marvel at how we could ever have dealt in shillings and pence, let alone hundredweights and stones, pints and gills, furlongs, feet and inches. Victorian educational games were, on the whole, not designed for such mental somersaults as this, but merely as a method of making the process of learning the three Rs (and a few other things) more palatable. Geographic games were the most popular: players had to do such difficult things as matching up the climate, main products, population, shape and name of the Gold Coast, British Guiana or some other part of what was then the great British Empire. Such games (and they came not only in the form of card games) are very popular among collectors today and, depending on date, subject-matter and condition, fetch as much as £5 or £6.

**Toys** It is a little difficult to separate games from toys, since their functions and meanings often overlap. However, such toys as building blocks of obvious prewar and earlier vintage, jigsaws of the same description (in that house we mentioned earlier, we found an educational jigsaw of 1806, well before the era of interlocking pieces, made up of all the counties of England—a great find for a collector), clockwork trains and their equipment, motorcars and ships are all of interest and potential value.

**Dolls** There is the classic case of a museum curator who was travelling through Gloucestershire not many years ago, and who went into a small general stores in one of the towns he came to. To his astonishment, he found that the shop still had much of its Victorian stock, some of it exactly as it had arrived from the wholesalers, even to the extent of being still wrapped and in its original boxes. Among the stock were rows of Victorian wax dolls, a find which caused a flurry of excitement among the people who care for such things.

Dolls of later periods (particularly those dealing with the two World Wars) are also sought after. At this time, most dolls were made of celluloid, later banned because of its inflammable qualities. Dolls are also collected as reference material for costume; this even applies, to a limited extent, to modern dolls in foreign costume.

*Eighteenth-century dolls' house*

**Dolls' houses** There is little about dolls' houses to add to what we have already said about dolls themselves. The same rules and the same criteria apply. Dolls' houses, however, have a wider appeal than dolls themselves; dolls tend to be exclusively the province of the female of the species, whereas dolls' houses, overlapping as they do into the realms of architecture, furniture and general social history, strike chords in many men as well. Quality and size vary enormously. The best are unbelievably good, perfect down to the last copper saucepan in the tiny kitchen, the miniature cat under the dining-room table, the microscopic candlestick on the mantel-shelf. Probably the finest of all, and an example of what can be achieved, is on view to the public at Windsor Castle. This belonged to Queen Mary. There are many far humbler versions that would find a ready market today, largely because the attention to detail that must go into the making of a dolls' house and its contents is the very thing which is missing from the present age of mass production; the admiration which such craftsmanship arouses in us is a strong card in the antique dealer's pack.

**Model soldiers**  There are few subjects which arouse such enthusiasm among collectors as militaria—soldiers and every-thing to do with them. Today's model soldiers are very different from those of even fifteen years ago; and 'Action Man' is a very far cry from the stiff and moustachioed upper lips of the Great War examples.

Model soldiers of any period up to and including the last war are valuable, and particularly the lead soldiers. There are many collectors of these, including several generals and military historians.

So far as condition is concerned, as long as the model is all there—that is, with both legs and arms and head—it does not matter too much if the paintwork is in poor condition; for one of the delights of the model soldier collectors is to restore to their model army the original uniforms in full glow-ing colour. As with all other types of collecting, some models are much rarer, and therefore more valuable, than others.

One model, loosely connected with soldiers, deserves special mention. The miniature copy of Queen Elizabeth's corona-tion coach made by Lesney in 1953 sold at the time of manu-facture for 2s 11d, complete with horses and footmen. Today it changes hands for £45.

**Books**  We have already, in Chapter 1, dealt in general terms with books. What we said there covers children's books also, but there are a few special features about juvenile books which should be mentioned. Firstly, anything to do with children—

or juvenilia as it is called—has its own special market, and commands more attention and better prices than adult material of similar type and date. Secondly, there are two classes of book which are particularly associated with children: educational books and annuals. Educational games and toys have already been mentioned, and books are equally popular, particularly where there are attractive embossed and gilded covers as mentioned in Chapter 1. Annuals, and similar books such as *The Boys' Book of Flying,* are also interesting to collectors when they cover periods of development—for example, submarines up to and including the Great War, aeroplanes for the same period and perhaps a little later, motor racing at Brooklands and so on.

**Optical toys** Since the last war, the cinema has largely given way to television as the main means of entertainment. But we often show each other our holiday slides, and if in the not-too-distant future they develop a new way of recording and showing our experiences—perhaps home movies coupled into the television set—then it may well be that these boxes of plastic squares holding pieces of coloured film will become bygones in their own right. Nothing stands still, and it is sometimes a chastening thought that the marvels of today will be laughed at as antiques tomorrow.

In early Victorian days, the cinema had not been invented, and neither, of course, had television. Even the still camera was not in general use. Home entertainment of this kind was centred on the magic lantern, an enclosed lamp with a projecting lens at one end. Early magic lanterns were huge and cumbersome, and the illumination was a single flame which cast a dim image on the wall. Magic lanterns continued to be made up to and including the years of the Great War, by which time of course they were powered by electric bulbs (to the great relief of the operators).

Magic lanterns themselves are unmistakable in appearance; most modern slide projectors in the cheaper range are almost exact miniature replicas. Many are certainly still hidden away in attics. However, of more interest than the magic lanterns themselves are the slides which were made for them.

The early ones were painted in oil colour on pieces of

glass about 2½ inches square. Another piece of glass the same size was then placed against the painted side, and the two pieces bound together round the edge with sticky tape. This was then inserted into a slide carrier between the light source and the lens of the magic lantern, and so projected on to the wall. An enormous variety of subjects was covered by these slides, both in the entertainment and in the educational fields. They were bought, as a rule, in wooden boxes holding anything up to a hundred. A single box might hold a set of 'Animals of the World' (some of the early ones, which were obviously painted by artists who had never seen some of the more unusual animals, are absolutely charming and eagerly sought after by collectors). 'Our Soldiers' or 'Our Navy' are typical of other popular subjects. Because the actual painting was protected in the sandwich of glass, these magic lantern slides have often survived in surprisingly good condition. When the dust has been blown off and the outer faces of the glass gently washed, they can reappear almost as good as new. As always, unusual subjects are more desirable, and will fetch better prices, than commonplace ones. For example, modern collectors are not much interested in the Victorian ideas of earlier periods of history; a set of slides showing the Pyramids and how the Egyptians buried their dead will arouse very little enthusiasm. But a set of Victorian slides showing the pleasure gardens of London—Vauxhall, Cremorne and so on—would cause a good deal of excitement, simply because it provides that vitally important ingredient for the historian–collector, contemporary evidence.

In the second half of the nineteenth century, a lot of effort was put into trying to make the images cast by the magic lantern actually move. The cine-camera and cine-projector were a long time ahead, and some of the early attempts were charmingly naïve. Collectors are always on the look out for:

*Animation strips* This was the earliest type, and the strips were up to 2 feet long. On the strips of glass (double glazed in the same way as the individual slides) were painted the successive stages of some lively action, such as a clown turning a somersault or a horse galloping. The animation was not very convincing, as the demonstrator merely pulled the slide along in front of the lamp, leaving each scene in view for a moment or two while he kept up a commentary. These animation strips should not be confused with the less desirable strips on which a whole number of different and unrelated scenes, or birds or animals, were painted; these were 'space savers', to avoid having to make an individual slide for each scene or figure. They are on the whole considerably later than the animated strips.

*Slipping slide*

*Slipping slides*  Most of these were larger than the individual magic lantern slides. They consisted of a wooden frame about 6 inches by 3, holding a sandwich of two or three sheets of glass of the same size. On these sheets of glass were painted different parts of a scene, and by pulling one across the other you could show two or three different stages of an action—as many stages as there were sheets of glass in fact. One that we found—alas not in an attic—shows in stage one a little man looking at himself in the mirror; in stage two a naughty child behind him holding an ass's head; and in stage three the ass looking at himself in the mirror.

*Lever and revolving slides*  These were slightly more sophisticated attempts at animation. Lever slides were of the same general construction as slipping slides, but instead of sliding the sheets of glass over one another to create the effect, you moved a little lever projecting from the side of the frame. The range of subjects which lever slides could animate was very limited—children on see-saws and ships heaving on the ocean were the usual ones. In the revolving slides, one circular sheet of glass was made to turn on top of the other by winding a handle at the side. Part of the scene was painted on one sheet and part on the other, so that you could achieve the effect of a waterwheel turning in a mill or a paddle steamer churning up the sea.

*Stereoscope*

Extremely popular as a means of home entertainment was the *stereoscope*. The principle of the stereoscope (still used, for example, in making relief maps from aerial photographs) is the same that has provided us with two eyes instead of one. The taking of two pictures of the same scene, from slightly different view points, gives a three-dimensional effect. Stereoscopic pictures were not made in the form of slides, but as pairs of (apparently) identical photographs pasted on to stiff card. Each pair was put into a special viewer—early models were handsome pieces of furniture made of mahogany and brass with nicely mounted glass lenses, one for each eye; in the early years of this century, a cheap standard form of semi-folding stereoscopic viewer was marketed.

Stereoscopes depended on photography for their success, because the effect was impossible to achieve in any other way.

They were probably at the height of their popularity during the First World War, when thousands of sets showing scenes at the Front, and in Europe generally, were produced. There are quite a lot of these wartime sets about, together with the standard folding stereoscope viewer, and the market is if anything overfull. Early viewers and views (for example, stereoscopic sets of the Boer War) are readily saleable.

The cinema depends on something called 'persistence of vision', which means simply that our brains hold, for a fraction of a second, an image of what our eyes have just seen. The cine-camera fools the brain by taking a series of still pictures, with a period of black-out between each. This principle was well known a hundred years ago. Two optical toys which made use of it were very popular among both adults and children. One was the *zoetrope*, which looks very like a table lamp complete with drum shade. But there is no lamp inside

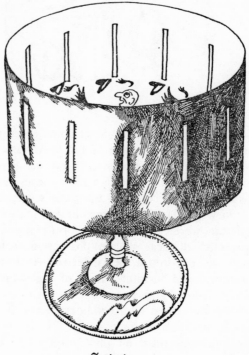

*Zoetrope*

and the shade has vertical slits cut in it all the way round. Inside the shade, facing in towards the centre, you put a specially-made strip of paper showing a number of stages in some animated scene, such as a dog jumping through a hoop. You then put the zoetrope in a good light, and spin the drum shade with your finger. If you bend down and look through the slits of the drum from the outside, you see, as each slit comes opposite a picture, a succession of images which blend together into a very lifelike moving scene. One hates to think of how many zoetropes have been thrown away as old lamps, and how many of the special strips of paper have been burnt because nobody knew what they were.

Similar strips of paper were used in another optical toy, the *praxinoscope*. Instead of slits round the side of the drum, there was a series of mirrors, fixed in a circle in the middle, which created the same effect. The advantage of the praxinoscope was that you did not have to bend down to peer through the slits; but in fact it was not quite as effective as the zoetrope.

There is a growing market among collectors for optical toys and other early forerunners of the cinema. Even the simplest toy of them all, the *thaumatrope* disc, is wanted. This is just a circular cardboard disc with two related pictures, one on each side—a parrot and a cage, or a ship and a bottle, for example. If the disc is held in front of you and twirled by the strings on each side, the two pictures come together into one, and you see the parrot in the cage, or the ship in the bottle.

**Scale models** Accurate scale models of such things as railway engines, motorcars or aeroplanes are fetching quite remarkable prices. But before all our readers snatch up their balsa-wood Spitfires and their cardboard *Mayflowers* and head for the nearest antique shop, let us be clear what we are talking about. The sort of scale-model railway engine that will reach Sotheby's (and this has recently happened) will have been made by a dedicated enthusiast and will probably have taken ten years to complete. It will be perfect in every detail down to the shape of the rivets; its scale will be accurate to one-hundredth of a millimetre; and it will work. Model collectors tend to specialize in one particular form of transport (or whatever it may be) and they are extremely fussy about the details. Nothing but perfection is really good enough Models built from kits will certainly not fit their bill, and in fact are probably worth nothing at all. But a brass and mahogany paddle-boat, or a perfect reproduction of Lindbergh's aeroplane *Spirit of St Louis,* or of Sir Malcolm Campbell's *Bluebird*—these are highly marketable. Collectors of such things are looking for absolutely authentic reproductions and for master-craftsmanship in their construction. Engineers and seamen were often expert at making models to these demanding standards, and a surprising number of them found that model-making was a satisfying and absorbing hobby. If your grandfather was a bridge builder or a ship's engineer, or equally if he spent his life in a lonely job like night-watchman or lighthouse keeper, it will be worth searching for models.

There is one particular class of model which is unique and of very high value. During the Napoleonic wars (1803–15) a large number of French prisoners were locked up in this country; Dartmoor prison was actually built for some of them. Many were craftsmen, and to earn money for extra food they developed a trade in making models fashioned from bone. The bone was actually part of their meat rations, but over the years it has become weathered until it looks like ivory. With this unlikely material, using hand-fashioned tools and endless patience, they made a very considerable number of the most exquisite models, mainly of ships. The rigging was fashioned from their own hair or horse-hair, and the models were put together with glue from the meat-bones and tiny nails fashioned from scraps of metal. If you possess a model ship which might be prisoner-of-war work, you should have it photographed and show the photograph to any antique dealer who has the sign of the British Antique Dealers Association in his window. The best models fetch four figures.

Equally as rare as the bone ships made by the prisoners of war are the models of such things as the guillotine, or forts with moving figures of soldiers. These were made both from bone and in straw marquetry work. They also made a number of smaller items in bone—little boxes, sets of dominoes, even packs of miniature playing cards pared from the bone. All these are extremely saleable, and are increasing in price all the time.

*Brass money box*

**Victorian money boxes** These are collectors' items, and the demand far outstrips the supply. Money boxes were made in wood, metal and pottery. Of these, by far the rarest are the pottery ones, for the simple reason that the only way of extracting the money from the pottery money box was to break it. Wooden ones and metal ones were fitted with some sort of semi-secret lid or opening, so that the contents could eventually be extracted and the box used again. Money boxes have been made in every conceivable shape and form, and obviously we cannot describe them all. But among the most desirable are the 'mechanical' boxes in which some sort of simple mechanism puts the coin into the box after it has been placed in a tray or receptacle. Typical of these is the American money box in the form of a rifleman aiming at a tree stump. One puts the coin on top of his rifle, presses a lever (which happens to be his foot) and the coin is shot by a spring into a slit in the tree stump. Another well-known semi-mechanical money box is the Negro's Head, in which the coin is placed in his hand and he lifts his arm and swallows it. (These, by the way, are being reproduced today.) We have ourselves collected from various odd sources (including attics) pottery money boxes in the shape of chests of drawers, houses and heads of well-known figures such as Robert Burns; wooden ones in the shape of castles and pillar boxes, and metal ones fashioned into—well, surprisingly enough, banks.

# 4
# War

War has a fascination for many collectors—indeed, there are many who concentrate on nothing else but war items, and some of them even restrict themselves to individual campaigns. As anyone who walks down Carnaby Street, or the Portobello Road on a Saturday morning, will be aware there is now a swing among pop fashion designers towards military uniform and insignia, and the trade papers are full of advertisements for material of this kind. We ourselves have mixed feelings about this. If old uniforms are going to rot in attics, being eaten to pieces by moths, then it is far better that they should come out and be put to use on a hippie's back. But we have seen some examples of really fine uniforms being misused, and this is sad. By all means look these things out from the attic—that is, after all, the whole purpose of this book—but having looked them out, take a little thought as to the best way of disposing of them; there are many markets for the more interesting items of militaria. For example, each regiment of the British Army (even the depleted number caused by amalgamations) maintains a museum, and curators of regimental museums are always delighted to hear of pieces of uniform—particularly early ones—and other regimental material such as campaign medals, or prints or other illustrations of uniforms being worn. Service museums are listed in the invaluable *Museums and Galleries* published annually in July by Index Publishers, price 25p. Only under exceptional circumstances will the regimental museum be in a position to buy such material, but as we have mentioned elsewhere, the treasures in your attic are not necessarily

*A modern (1930) woodcut by*
*Harry Butler*

*Woven silk bookmarks by*
*Thomas Stevens and other makers*

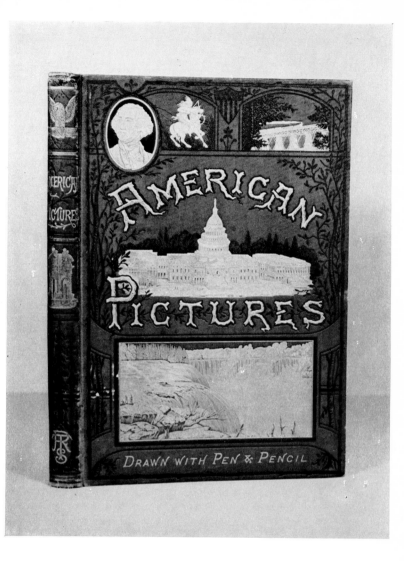

*A fine decorative book cover –
with American interest – c. 1885*

*An early-nineteenth-century*
*portable microscope*

counted in monetary terms. Gifts, or items on long loan, are likely to be displayed with the donor's name, which ensures at least a small piece of immortality.

Most people who have actually taken part in a war, whether they were fighting at the Front or undergoing bombing and rationing at home, are only too anxious to forget all about it once the war is over. For this reason, personal souvenirs are not nearly as commonplace as one might think. In fact, souvenirs of the First World War are far more plentiful than those of the Second. People have moved about so much since the end of the last war, and there has been such a revolution in housing, that many war souvenirs have gone into the dust-bin long before they would otherwise have done.

In those attics where such things have been stored away, this is what to look for:

*Ceremonial Nazi dagger*

**Nazi souvenirs** German uniforms (Italians ones are not nearly so marketable) including steel helmets, medals and badges, particularly Iron Crosses and swastika badges, officers' caps, ceremonial daggers (ornamented with swastikas), in fact anything which is obviously of Nazi origin. Try an advertise-

ment under a box number in *Exchange and Mart*, or take
them to one of the specialist militaria shops in the Portobello
Road on Saturday. Not mentioned in the list above are guns
—rifles, revolvers and bigger and more unpleasant things.
These should have been handed in to the police long ago.
If you do come across a gun or a pistol, treat it with the
utmost care and get your local policeman to come and take
it away. Unless you know about firearms, it is dangerous
to play about with them, and it is in any case probably illegal
to sell them.

**Civilian mementoes** Pieces of shrapnel that fell on your
house in 1941 or bits of the German aeroplane that came
down in the field nearby are still unconsidered items among
collectors. No doubt there are enlightened people who are
starting to gather such things together, but on the whole
there is no market for them. Keep them for twenty years and
there will be. Similar things from the First World War—
particularly such special items as pieces of shot-down
Zeppelins—are certainly collected, however.

Those people who kept ration books, identity cards, gas
masks and other civilian souvenirs from the First World War
have been able to find a ready market for them; the same has
started to be true of similar objects from the Second World
War.

**Shell and bullet work** During the First World War,
when there were very long periods of complete stagnation
in the fighting and for months on end soldiers had nothing to
do but keep themselves alive, quite a considerable industry
grew up making things from shell cases, spent bullets, wrecked
vehicles and all the paraphernalia of the battlefield. There
was no shortage of material. And there was also no shortage
of machinery in the workshops to deal with those parts of the
manufacturing process that were too difficult to achieve by
hand. Millions of ashtrays formed from the base of shell cases;
thousands of cigarette lighters from cartridge cases or pairs of
regimental buttons; and hundreds of model aeroplanes and
tanks (often made from materials supplied by burnt-out or
shot-down originals) were turned out as souvenirs for admir-

*Part of propeller from German aircraft shot down over Arras, 1915*

ing relatives—or, no doubt, for sale by enterprising Tommies. These metal mementoes are often engraved with dates or places—Arras, Ypres and so on—and a very considerable number of them are also decorated with scrolls and patterns formed from a succession of dots punched in the brass. This is almost a trademark, and one suspects that a complete base workshop found itself with nothing to do and turned its whole productive capacity to making these souvenirs! At all events there are a great many of them.

Some are more specialized, and as a result more interesting. We recently picked up the brass-bound tip of a mahogany propeller, cut from a German plane shot down over Arras and suitably inscribed. Into a hole cut in the wood of the propeller was an embroidered silk picture of the ruins of Arras itself. This was in a junk shop, but it had obviously come recently from somebody's attic.

*Princess Mary's giftbox, 1914*

**Princess Mary's giftbox**  In 1914, Princess (later Queen) Mary sent to every soldier serving in France at Christmas a brass box, about 6 inches by 4 inches by 1 inch, embossed with her portrait and a suitable inscription, and containing cigarettes and chocolate together with a Christmas message. Quite a lot of these have survived, but very few of them—not surprisingly—still have the contents untouched. Under the hinged lid was a second lid, sealed down to keep the inside airtight. Unopened tins of this kind are worth several pounds.

**Silk maps**  During the last war, air crew were issued with fine maps, printed on silk and housed in a waterproof bag, to help them reach safety if they were shot down over enemy territory. These maps are now quite rare.

There is of course a great mass of material which is attributable to both wars, and it would be impossible to mention all the categories, let alone the individual items. Much of this material has been put away, never to be looked at again, and it is a pity that owners and collectors should not have the opportunity of benefiting mutually.

There is however one major class of war souvenirs which should be mentioned, and that is:

**Souvenir china**  Nearly all of this comes from the First World War, with the result that souvenir china of the Second World War is particularly valuable. With some difficulty we have discovered a few of the latter: for example a pottery bulldog wearing a tin hat; and a teapot marked 'War against Hitlerism. This souvenir teapot was made for Dyson and Horsfall of Preston to replace aluminium stocks taken over for allied armaments 1939.'

First World War souvenir china is a good deal commoner. Among the types which are looked for are plates, dishes, jugs, teapots and other domestic utensils decorated in a sepia colour with prints of Bruce Bairnsfather's famous humorous pictures of Life in the Trenches (already mentioned in the section on postcards); and *crested china*.

There can be few people who can be unfamiliar with the

*Second World War souvenir – 'Hitler's terror'*

crude little models in white china, almost invariably decorated with the crest of some seaside (or occasionally inland)
town, which were sold by the million in the period 1910
to 1939. They originally cost 3d or 6d, and had no pretensions
to artistic merit. Among them were a vast number of little
urns and vases and pots, and these are practically valueless
(except for those made by Goss—see below). However, during
and immediately after the First World War most of the
manufacturers turned out little models of objects connected
with the war, and these are now eagerly collected. All the
different kinds of British tanks, aeroplanes, Zeppelins, anti-
aircraft guns of the Royal Naval Air Service, war memorials,
models of Nurse Edith Cavell (shot by the Germans), models
of a hearth labelled 'We've kept the home fires burning', an
old kit bag suitably labelled, machine guns, sticky bombs,
trench lamps—there are several hundred varieties, all of them
of great interest. Unusual ones—such as a model of the

*Lusitania*—will sell for up to £5. Many of them have printed inscriptions on the bottom such as 'Model of Tommy in his dugout', or (on a model of a submarine) 'E.I. Commander Noel Lawrence large German transport sunk July 30th 1915 German cruiser torpedoed August 19th 1915.'

There were several manufacturers who made these models, including firms called Arcadian, Carlton, Grafton and Shelley. The only one to look out for particularly among pieces of souvenir china is W. H. Goss. This firm made only a few war models, and these sell at a very distinct premium over those of other manufacturers. Goss also made a large number of crested china models unconnected with the war (houses, pots and other things) and these also fetch comparatively high prices. If you find in your attic a little Goss model of a house or cottage (they vary from 2 to 9 inches long and include replicas of Anne Hathaway's Cottage, Burns's cottage, etc.) advertise it, all by itself, in *Exchange and Mart* or one of the antiques magazines. It will be worth it. Values range from £12 for a small model of a common subject, such as Shakespeare's birthplace, to £50 upwards for a model of, say, Dr Samuel Johnson's birthplace at Lichfield.

**Prints, posters and photographs**    Original examples of the famous poster showing General Kitchener pointing his finger and saying 'The Army Needs You' are important collectors' items; enthusiasts also search for the many other posters which were produced during the First World War (particularly) to urge the country on to better things. Second World War posters—such things as 'Careless Talk Costs Lives' and 'Dig for Victory'—are also collected. Photographs of Second World War generals are of no value at the moment, although photographs of such figures as Orde Wingate, who commanded the Chindits in Burma and became a legendary figure in his own short lifetime, are an exception. First World War generals are also something of a drug on the market, except where they have been incorporated into the very handsomely coloured large prints that were fashionable in those days. These are usually covered with gaily decorated flags, pictures of our warships and tanks and other enthusiastic and patriotic symbols. Many were framed and hung on the walls of thous-

*First World War – embroidered panel showing the flags of our allies*

ands of houses in England as a reminder of the victory which was to come. Even more eagerly collected today are the large embroidered pictures, sometimes as large as 2 feet square, showing (as a rule) flags of the allies surrounding a small frame in which a photograph of an absent serving son could be put.

# 5
# Luggage and clothes

Luggage has been put in the attic from time immemorial. Much of it is still there, no longer wanted. Unfortunately, most of it is quite unsaleable except at junk prices. People travel more and more, and what they need is strong, light luggage that will go into aeroplanes. Victorian luggage was certainly strong, but one large leather case from that period, empty, would probably take up most of your air baggage allowance.

No, the sad thing is that attic luggage is almost totally unwanted, and might just as well remain doing its existing job of holding other things. There are, however, one or two exceptions.

**Cabin trunks**  Those huge, handsome, brass-bound trunks with which one set off to start a new life in India or some other far-flung outpost of the British Raj are converted these days into quite substantial pieces of furniture. It all seems rather sad, and unless you really need the space or the comparatively small amount of money which will be offered you, cabin trunks would probably be happier in the attics of their own families.

**Gladstone bags**  Gladstone bags, like outsize cricket bags in solid leather, have period interest and the demand will increase from the present moderately low level.

**Helmet tins**  These will find a much more ready market. Like cabin trunks, they were designed to go out with their owners to hot climates where the elaborate headgear which the military man (depending on the regiment he was in) wore was likely to suffer from the penetrating damp and the devastating insects. Some of these containers are very oddly shaped indeed. The helmet tin had to follow exactly the shape of the headgear itself, and one can therefore find everything from the reasonably simple cocked-hat shape to helmet tins intended for some of the more exotic kinds of cavalry headgear. The owner's name and regiment will almost invariably be painted on the tin somewhere, either inside or out—sometimes both. If the original cap or helmet is inside the tin, so much the better.

**Clothes** Inside one of the trunks in the attic, there may well be a pile of old clothes. As a general rule, there is nothing more depressing in the world than a bundle of unwanted clothes, and a visit to any jumble sale will convince those who doubt it. However, there are many occasions when old clothes have been deliberately and carefully stored away. They may be of sentimental value—uniforms have already been mentioned; wedding dresses, christening robes and babies' clothes are other possibilities—or they may form a fancy-dress collection. This was very common in larger houses; fancy-dress games were extremely popular in Victorian and Edwardian times (and in many houses still are) and a special trunk of clothes was kept for the business of dressing up. Some most surprising finds have been made in such miscellaneous collections. The difficulty is to know what you have got. Costume collecting is a specialized business, and the things which are wanted by collectors are often the very things you would throw away on the first sorting through— such things as underclothes and corsets, particularly of pre-Victorian vintage, are rare and of great value. Anyone who thinks there is a collection of interesting and worthwhile costume in his attic should read one of the following books: *Victorian Costumes and Costume Accessories* by Anne Buck (Herbert Jenkins, 1961), and *Costume in Pictures* by Phillis Cunnington (Studio Vista, 1964); or better still should pay a visit to the Museum of Costume at Bath or the costume collection at the Victoria and Albert Museum in London.

Anything of Georgian or earlier date, especially complete outfits and children's clothes, is of particular interest to collectors. The danger is that the clothes may have been altered at a later date to make the original more fashionable or more suitable for fancy-dress; if the alterations are major ones, the value of the costume will have been destroyed.

Some types of costume have survived in far greater numbers than others. For example, with the rigorous rules for mourning which Victorian society demanded, there have survived a very large number of dresses and outer garments in black; unless they are of exceptional quality these are of little interest to either museums or collectors. Again, a heavily boned Georgian corset will be of far greater interest to a collector than finely embroidered christening robes, as the latter were kept by so many families.

One useful tip—turn the clothes inside-out and see if the stitching is by machine or by hand. The lock-stitch sewing machine came into general use only in the 1860s, which gives a rough date check.

Other things which are loosely connected with clothes and costume, and which are quite likely to have found their way to the attic, include *sticks, umbrellas* and *parasols*. Umbrellas, designed specifically to keep off the rain (as opposed to the sun) came into use in the middle of the eighteenth century, at which time they were objects of ridicule. Early examples were much larger than our modern umbrella, and had heavy whalebone ribs supporting a huge cotton cover, with a very long supporting stick.

The parasol, intended to keep the sun from a lady's face, and also as a weapon in the war of the sexes, came into its own in about 1800. Some of the early examples were real works of art, with sticks and handles of polished steel, carved wood or ivory, silk or muslin covers and a wealth of fringe.

Men's sticks are on the whole the most readily saleable of the three. Some are quite straightforward, and rely for their good looks and usefulness on handsome materials and elegant proportions. Sticks in which the handle is formed into a dog's head, sometimes in ivory, are very popular among collectors; so are those formed into a whistle. There are also examples where an enormous amount of care and trouble has been lavished to achieve a striking effect—carving in ivory or solid wood was something carried to extraordinary lengths on walking-sticks.

Above all, there is a distinct element of the unexpected. There was a vogue in Victorian times for concealing other things inside a walking-stick. It might be a sword, in which case a twist of the handle and a moderate tug will reveal the blade inside; or it might be a glass phial to hold about a quarter of a pint of brandy—for medicinal purposes, of course. Some dedicated gambling men even kept a set of dice in the handle of their walking sticks, and there are also examples of collapsible pipes being hidden similarly.

One walking-stick in an attic is unlikely to be anything more than it seems, but a bundle may well contain one or more sticks with something interesting hidden away.

Mention should also be made of the most valuable kind of walking-stick, which is the eighteenth-century walking staff. This is much longer than a walking-stick and has no turned-over handle—it is a straight cane, often of fine wood, and equally often lavishly decorated. These are occasionally made in more than one piece, which screw together, and conceal a space for a container of some liquid comforter.

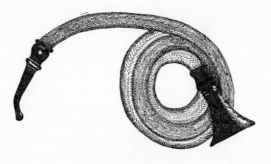

*Victorian ear trumpet*

**Ear trumpets**    These unwieldy Victorian forerunners of the modern hearing aid are typical of the sort of dress-accessory which collectors look for. There were both rigid (like a small gramophone horn) and flexible models. We were ourselves delighted to find one of the latter in a London junk shop, the trumpet and the earpiece connected by a long length of flexible tube and the whole affair contained in a little velvet bag: and surprisingly efficient it is.

**Hats**  Among hats which are sought after are straw boaters, collapsible top hats (known as opera hats, crush hats or gibuses), solar topees, military headgear from the Great War and earlier, women's country bonnets, and such specialized headgear as motoring hats (both male and female), veils and policemen's helmets (acquired perhaps by an undergraduate forebear).

**Hatpins**  These fearsome weapons up to a foot long, with which Edwardian women used to secure their hats to their heads, are now collected. They were made in enormous variety, and the more extravagant the decoration, the more desirable they are.

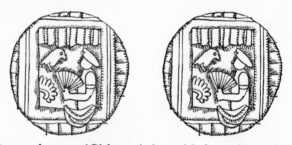

*Art Nouveau buttons – 'Girl at window with fan and parrot' pattern*

**Buttons**  Buttons are in the early years of being collected; in her book *Buttons* (Studio Vista), published in 1968, Diana Epstein says 'they are nearly unexplored territory and provide many opportunities for being there first'. The demand is growing rapidly, however, and there is now at least one shop in London which sells nothing but old buttons. Under no circumstances should buttons be cut from a garment to which they are attached, because to a costume historian the combination of a particular kind of garment (or a particular kind of material) with the buttons can be of great importance in dating them accurately. But there can be few houses that don't have a button box for replacing fasteners that come off clothes; here there may be treasures. The materials used and the variety of design are infinite, and in this book we can only recommend you to specialized works such as *Buttons* or *The Button Sampler* by Lilian Smith Albert and Jane Ford Adams (Gramercy Publishing Company of America, 1951); or a visit to 'The Button Queen' in St Christopher's Place, London W.1.

**Sporting clothes**   These are of particular interest to costume collectors. Motoring hats have already been mentioned. In the early days of motoring—around the turn of the century—drivers also wore complete enveloping ankle-length dust coats, gauntlets and goggles to make sure they were protected from the clouds of dust that the motorcars threw up. Prints of about the same period show the uniforms which sportsmen and sportswomen wore—cycling outfits consisting of tight knickerbockers and long stockings for men, golfing clothes, tennis clothes, shooting clothes, riding habits (side-saddle for women, of course). As an example, croquet dresses of the 1860s have been discovered, provided with special drawstrings to enable the lady to raise the floor-length skirt sufficiently high to make her shot. The decorative petticoat thus revealed is an essential part of the costume.

**Fans**   No Victorian lady would venture far in summer, or in the evening at any time of year, without her fan. What a pity it is that this elegant habit has disappeared: not only was the fan a sensible idea and a handsome accessory, but in the hands of an expert it was a formidable feminine weapon. Fans continued to be made in this country certainly up to the beginning of the last war, and they are still being made today in great quantities in Japan. The cheap, garishly painted fan mounted on slivers of bamboo or other cheap wood is of no interest to collectors, and of no value. Early fans leave one in no doubt that they were important dress accessories, both by the materials they were made of and the care that was taken in their construction and decoration. Carved ivory, mother of pearl, papier mâché, lacquered or japanned wood, or finely carved hardwoods—these are the

*Ivory fan*

indications of quality fan sticks. The fan itself (the material connecting the sticks, that is) was of silk, lace, kid or feathers in good quality examples. Finally, fans of any quality always had their own case or box, and although a case may have disappeared in the course of time, its presence adds distinctly to the value of the fan.

**Footwear** On the whole, footwear is not wanted by the antique trade. But there are, as always, exceptions. For example pattens (wooden soles with an extra iron support fixed

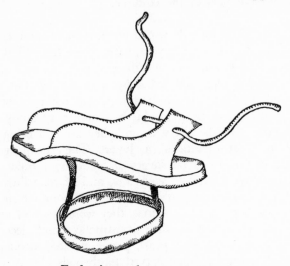

*Early nineteenth-century pattens*

to the bottom, often in the shape of a ring, and worn by men and women in the street to keep their feet out of the Georgian and early Victorian filth) are certainly collectors' items. But otherwise, even such elegant things as beautifully-polished riding boots are of little monetary value. Oddly enough, of far more interest to the trade are some of the minor items connected with footwear: Georgian cut-steel or silver shoe buckles; or a folding bootjack set, consisting of a collapsible wooden heel gripper containing a pair of metal and ivory pullers that went through the loops at the top of the boot. The metal pullers helped you on with the boot, the wooden jack helped you off with it. There are also to be found such unusual items as an eighteenth-century ostler's companion, the wall-mounted piece of equipment used for stretching, drying and polishing riding boots.

**Foreign dress and costume** This is beyond the scope of this book, but you should be aware of the possibilities. We have personal experience of some nineteenth-century Maori feather costumes, brought from New Zealand before the First World War and used until recently by the children of the family for dressing-up games. Luckily they were still in comparatively good condition, and they have been bought by a collector for a handsome sum. As we have said elsewhere, a knowledge of your own family history will again be your best guide in deciding whether unexplained items of dress and clothing in your attic trunks are potentially valuable or not. If your great-grandfather was a missionary in West Africa, or joined one of the gold rushes, or served on the North-west frontier, then you have reason to take a close look at what you find.

It might be appropriate at this point to mention the enormous quantity of material which came back from India as the result of two hundred years of British domination of the continent. In that time millions of British subjects travelled to and fro, on military service, in the civil service or in commerce, and every one of them brought back souvenirs. As a general rule, very little of this is of any value. Carvings of elephants, brass trays—there must be thousands of them scattered in homes throughout the British Isles. Apart from the obvious relics of the early days of the British in India—for example, any authenticated memento of the Indian Mutiny is a collectors' item—there is little of this material which is readily saleable. There are some things which, perhaps unexpectedly, are nevertheless wanted. There was a strange macabre habit of turning elephants' feet into wastepaper baskets and umbrella stands; these fetch extraordinarily high prices. Also wanted are *uncarved* ivory elephant tusks, good tiger skins (and to a lesser extent good skins of other big cats) and, strangest of all, rhinoceros horn. There are regular advertisements in *Exchange and Mart* for rhinoceros horns. The reason is that many Asiatic and African races regard powdered rhinoceros horn as a powerful aphrodisiac.

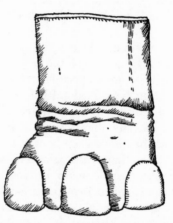

*Waste paper basket made from elephant's foot*

**Sports equipment** We have already mentioned sports clothes. Much of the equipment for playing games has changed very considerably in the course of the last hundred years or so. For example, at Wimbledon in the last two or three years, steel racquets have become almost standard among the top players. Compare these with the solid, nearly heart-shaped wooden racquets of the pre-Great War period, and one can see how technology and fashion have changed the face of sport. There is, as yet, little interest in early sports equipment. This is a great pity, because the result is that most

*A selection of collectable
postcards – embroidered silk,
1915 costume, Louis Wain, early
motoring*

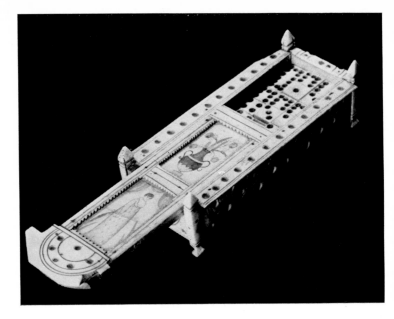

*French prisoner-of-war bone domino box*

*Crested china with first-World-War interest*

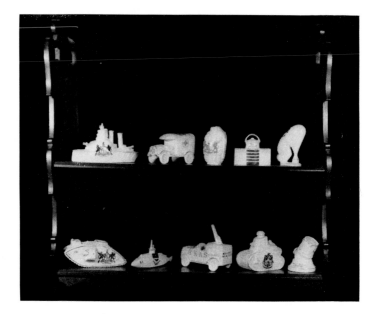

*A pair of tempera pictures showing*
*Vesuvius by day and night*

*Pyrograph picture, 'The Gipsy', by I. W. Wells, 1862*

*A mosaic of Victorian song covers*

*Baxter print entitled 'The
Hop Garden', published 1856*

*A fine pair of Sheffield plate candlesticks on a Victorian what-not*

*A collection of Wemyss pottery,*
*in a Georgian chemist's shop*
*display cabinet*

*Dairy advertisement model on a*
*cast-iron pub table*

of the interesting material will disappear before it can be collected together. It is past time that a proper museum of sport and sporting equipment was established. Who has Bobby Locke's golfing cap, and where are Jesse Owen's running shoes?

The one major exception in Britain's general lack of interest in early sporting items is in the cricket field. This, our national sport, arouses extraordinary passions and extraordinary enthusiasms. There are many specialist collectors of early cricket material, and there is therefore keen competition for interesting items. Pottery figures made in Staffordshire in the mid and late nineteenth century are mentioned in Chapter 9. Early cricketing prints and pictures, association items connected with such scintillating names as W. G. Grace, Fuller Pilch, the Foster brothers (and increasingly such modern giants as Bradman, or Freddie Trueman) are likely to fetch good prices; so are cricketing pictures, particularly

*Croquet set*

if they show early scenes of matches where the players still wore top hats or where the even earlier curved bat was in use. Old cricketing gear, bats, pads and so on, are of virtually no value, and would best be given, with the owner's blessing, to a boys' club or scout troop. *Croquet* remains popular among a limited section of the population. There is therefore a steady demand for old croquet sets. New ones (they are still made in almost exactly the same form) are extremely expensive, with the result that old ones in good condition fetch quite surprising prices. Advertisements for croquet sets are quite often to be seen in such magazines as *Country Life* or *The Field* and in the *Country Gentlemen's Magazine*.

**Jewellery** No one is likely to find a diamond tiara or the Imperial Russian crown in his attic. There are, however, many items of costume jewellery, mainly from the Victorian era, which are now in demand by collectors. Most pieces of this kind have been put away in boxes labelled 'Grandmother's odds and ends' or some such. In forgotten collections of this kind you may find *mourning jewellery*.

When Prince Albert, Queen Victoria's consort, died in 1861 the Queen decreed that only jet jewellery should be worn in her presence. This fashion (which lasted for the rest of her long life) was taken up by women throughout the country and practically every middle-class home in the country boasted a necklace, ear-rings or brooch made of jet. These are not only now collected, but they are also starting to be worn in their own right.

The Victorians in any case (and to a lesser extent the Georgians) had an absolute passion for mourning. When even a comparatively distant relative died, all relations plunged themselves into mourning for set periods and in accordance with strict rules of etiquette. Mourning jewellery was quite a standard part of the formula, particularly among the better-off families. Rings, enamelled in black and gold, with the name of the departed and the date of death, were worn by close relatives in the eighteenth century. More unusual are the similar rings enamelled in white instead of black. These almost invariably were made in memory of a dead child or

66

young person. Sometimes these rings were decorated with skulls and urns as reminders of mortality.

Some very charming hair jewellery was made, not always for mourning purposes. We have occasionally found, as quite unconsidered items in boxes of old trinkets, watch cords and ear-rings made from plaited hair, sometimes with gold or silver end-pieces. Locks of hair were also made into lockets, or sometimes plaited into attractive patterns under glass or crystal to form the bezel of a ring. Certainly the ultimate in this type of slightly macabre (to modern taste) form of decoration was the 'tree of life' pattern. Here, hair from several generations of one family was worked into the shape of a tiny tree so that (for example) the trunk of the tree would be formed from grandfather's grey hair; shadows with father's black hair; and so on down to the leaves made from baby's golden curls.

*Mid-nineteenth-century mourning jewellery*

Mourning items of all kinds are very popular among specialist collectors, and good examples of mourning jewellery are always sure of a ready market.

The other class of minor jewellery which should be mentioned, as it was extremely popular when it first came out and is almost equally sought after, is in the style known as Art Nouveau. It first appeared in the 1880s, and was a completely new concept in art and decoration which

67

embraced pictures, furniture, architecture, clothes, books and decorations as well as jewellery. It lasted until the outbreak of the First World War. Art Nouveau is impossible to describe accurately in a single paragraph; readers who suspect, after reading the next few sentences, that they have some examples of Art Nouveau costume jewellery should consult one of the many books on the subject such as *The World of Art Nouveau* by Martin Battersby (Arlington Books, 1968). The style has a clear ancestor in Japanese art, is typified by swirling, disturbing lines and forms, and a great emphasis upon nature – flowers, insects, birds, rushes, grasses. It was a complete reversal of the earlier Victorian Gothic style, which had been full of sombre, angular heaviness. The whole style of Art Nouveau was a leaping-up out of the earth; where human figures appear they are mysterious or satanic, the very opposite of our normal humdrum existence. In Art Nouveau jewellery, the peacock was one of the favourite designs. Among the best known designers of jewellery were Emile Gallé, René Lalique and the Czech artist Alphonse Mucha.

*Art Nouveau brooch by René Lalique*

# 6

# Pictures

It is almost impossible to believe that there is a single attic in the country that has not got at least one picture stacked against the wall. Is it worth £1,000 or even £100,000—or nothing? What sort of a picture is it? Is it even a picture at all, or a print? All these are questions which ought to be answered, and even if the answers do not produce an instant fortune for you, you will learn something about pictures (and in Chapter 7 about prints as well) which you may not have known before.

Pictures may be produced in all sorts of different materials and we shall be talking about most of them in the following pages. The thing that decides whether something in a frame is a picture or not is that it was created *by hand,* and that there is *only one.* A picture that has been painted by hand, whether that hand belonged to Rembrandt or Great Aunt Sarah, is an individual work of art. If it is reproduced, it has to be done by some mechanical means such as photography, and the result is not a picture, but a print, or in modern terms, a reproduction. This is why individual pictures by well-known artists fetch such enormous sums—the buyer knows that he has something that nobody else in the world has got. There must be millions of reproductions of Gainsborough's *Blue Boy,* as prints, Christmas cards or book illustrations. But if you want to see the real Gainsborough's *Blue Boy,* there is only one and you have to go to the Huntingdon Collection, California.

It is therefore absolutely vital that before deciding you have a masterpiece in your attic, you establish whether it is in fact a picture or one of the many forms of reproduction.

Pictures are painted by hand (although among modern painters there are more unconventional methods such as riding a bicycle over the canvas) and on to a suitable surface. Probably you are most familiar with the idea of oil paint applied to canvas, since this is how most of the great paintings that we see in art galleries were produced. But pictures can be painted on (among other things) wood, glass, china and paper, and there are many examples of all of these in the famous collections of the world. Oil paint is only one of a number of substances which can be applied to a surface to make a picture. Others include watercolours (the paint-boxes of our youth), gouache (which is merely watercolour to which Chinese white has been added to make the colours opaque), and tempera, which uses a mixture of egg-yolk and watercolour.

You must then be careful to distinguish pencil drawings, which may or may not have been coloured by means of water-colours afterwards; and pen-and-ink drawings (easily confused with prints) which may have been similarly coloured.

As you can see, the subject is full of difficulties and complications, and the first thing you must do in trying to decide what you are looking at is to reduce the problem to its simplest terms. First of all, look round the edges of the picture. If there is any form of printing or printed words (usually along the bottom edge) then the picture is not an original, but a print. Such Latin abbreviations as *delin.* or *del.* and *sculpt.* provide definite information that the subject is a print and not a picture; they stand, respectively, for 'drawn' and 'engraved' and the name of the artist and the engraver follows the words. If you find such printing, then you know where you are. If you don't find any printing at all, it still does not mean that the 'treasure' you have found is necessarily a picture. It could still be a print, for many types of print (particularly those drawn and engraved by well-known artists) do not have such clear clues. It is also possible that the printing is hidden behind the frame or mount.

We will deal with the different kinds of print, and how to recognize them, in Chapter 7. Let us for a moment concentrate on pictures.

**Oil paintings** These are the easiest to recognize. Oil paint has a definite thickness, and indeed some artists used it more like putty than paint. You can often see this thickness of paint, particularly on highlights such as crests of waves, or patches of bright sunshine. Another very important clue to oil paintings is the way in which the surface of the picture has cracked. Because of the different kinds of canvas and paint used in the different periods, seventeenth-century oil paintings and eighteenth-century ones have cracked in quite a different way. Seventeenth-century craquelure (as it is known) tends to go in more or less rectangular forms; the craquelure of eighteenth-century oil paintings is more likely to be in the form of spiders' webs.

It is wise to have an extremely careful look at the back of any picture you find, before trying to make up your mind as to what it is and whether it is valuable. The date, subject-matter and artist are sometimes (particularly if the picture is a good one) clearly written on the back of the frame on a label. If the label is missing, or if there are no details at all written on the back (a little attention with a soft brush and a duster may bring up hidden writing) one is driven to looking for further clues. There may be a signature on the front (usually on the bottom right-hand corner or left-hand corner) and the name can be looked up in *Graves' Dictionary of Artists 1760–1893* at the library. If the artist is mentioned in the dictionary then you have certainly found something that is worth money. You may not be as lucky as the late Sir Albert Richardson, Past President of the Royal Academy, who seemed to find really valuable paintings hidden away in junk shops or attics at the rate of about one a year. But of course he had a lifetime of experience behind him and he knew exactly what he was looking for.

If there is no signature and no other clues, you must try to decide on the quality of the painting. This is a much more difficult matter as it involves individual taste, but there are a great many bad pictures that have been painted and a great many of these carefully framed and hung in positions of importance. If after due consideration you think your oil painting is a good one, take it in the first instance to your local art shop, or to the curator of your local art gallery if there is one reasonably near by (museums these days often have collections of paintings as well as other exhibits, and there is usually a member of the staff who has at least some idea of relative merits).

Subject-matter can be important in determining the value of a painting, all other factors being equal. Pictures of ships are always popular, probably because we are an island people. But beware of the 'Windjammer rounding the Horn' type of picture which is almost invariably modern. Landscapes too are well received—if you want to know what a really good landscape looks like, go and see some of Constable's paintings at the National Gallery.

Portraits are, on the whole, very difficult to sell. Any original oil painting found in an attic and depicting a man or a woman is almost certain to be a portrait of some member of your own family, and such a picture in any case ought to be hanging on your own walls. It will be of very little interest to anybody else (unless there are other branches of your own family) and therefore of almost no value. The only exception might be if you had some forebear who was *really* well known —a statesman perhaps, or a famous beauty, or even a notorious murderer. Authenticated portraits of such figures would command good prices—but they should still really be hanging on your own walls.

**Watercolours** Watercolour pictures are almost invariably painted on paper. Those of you who remember your early efforts with paintboxes will be able to recognize the techniques. The colours are mixed with water to produce a wash, and the result is so thin on the paper that you cannot really see any substance in the colour. Watercolour pictures tend to be smaller than oil paintings, although it is true that one occasionally finds very small oil paintings and very large watercolours. Because the painting is done on paper, you see none of the graininess or knobbiness that one associates with canvas.

Watercolours are a particularly English form of art; a great many amateur artists during the eighteenth and nineteenth centuries went abroad and took their artists' materials with them. The result is that portfolios of watercolours quite

72

often turn up, some of them containing work of high quality. It is not likely that you will come across work by any of the really well known artists in this medium—such figures as John Constable, Peter de Wint or David Cox—but English watercolours are so popular among collectors that competent work by unknown artists is often readily saleable. If you find a signed watercolour (and a lot of them are) the three-volume *Dictionary of Water-colour Painting in Britain* lists all the better-known British artists in this medium. If your local library does not have a copy, they will get it for you.

One or two words of warning which apply particularly to watercolours. They are very delicate things, especially if they are unframed. Paper tears and gets dirty very easily. If a watercolour has become dirty through layers of dust, do not under any circumstances try to clean the dirt off with anything more drastic than a feather duster. Picture cleaning is a highly specialized skill, and the well-meaning use of a rubber, a scraper or even a duster has ruined many a picture for ever. Water, which includes a damp atmosphere, is of course death to any picture painted in watercolour. So, in the long run, is light; no watercolour should ever be exposed to strong sunlight because the colours fade. You will find in all museums and art galleries that good watercolours are always hung in positions where they do not receive direct light, or else they are provided with curtains or covers.

Portraits in watercolour are comparatively rare. Most English watercolours are of landscapes and seascapes, subjects which respond very well to being captured in this particular medium. As in the case of oil paintings, seascapes and pictures of ships are particularly popular among collectors.

**Gouache** This is a French term used to describe water-colours to which Chinese white has been added to make the paints opaque instead of transparent. The technique of painting is quite different, for gouache colours dry to quite a different shade (much lighter in fact) than they were when they were applied wet. This material was much more popular on the Continent than it was in England, and it is true to say that with a few exceptions, gouaches are continental (mainly French) and watercolours are English. One way to tell the difference between a watercolour and a gouache is to look at the highlights—the white parts, such as the reflections on water, snow, white cuffs on portraits, things like that. In a watercolour, these parts will be plain white paper, without any watercolour paint on it at all. In a gouache, however, these highlights will actually be painted in with white paint, and you will be able to see the brushmarks.

**Tempera**    Tempera is a cousin of watercolours and gouaches, but it uses egg-yolk (just the plain, simple yolk of an ordinary egg) mixed with the watercolour paint to produce its luminous effect. During the late eighteenth and most of the nineteenth centuries, when people went off to travel round Europe, recording their impressions by means of poetry, pictures and drawings, a tremendous number of foreign views were produced in this medium by amateur artists. There is a great vogue for them today, particularly those which show views of the Bay of Naples and Vesuvius in eruption, by day or by night. (A great many of these were also produced locally.) Tempera pictures of sailing craft of all kinds were painted in great quantity also, and these too are worthwhile collectors' items.

Wood has already been mentioned as a material on which paintings were done. But there is of course wood—and wood. Most of the earliest paintings in the world (almost invariably religious subjects) were done on panels of hard wood. If you see them in the great galleries, you will find that the wood panel has very often split or warped. From the time that canvas was generally introduced as an artist's surface, wood went out of favour. But various wood and wood-like materials reappeared in the nineteenth century, and are still used in some quantity today. Artist's board is a specially prepared, slightly grainy surface which is based on plywood. This is extremely common as a base for modern pictures. A vast number of modern pictures of all kinds have also been painted on ordinary hardboard. There should be little difficulty in telling the difference between the hard unyielding surface of wood (in all its forms) and the flexible surface of canvas. Watercolours were never painted on anything but paper.

Two other matters should be mentioned before we move on to the equally important (for the attic treasure-seeker) subject of prints. What about damage; and what about frames?

**Damage**  Whether damage is a question of vital importance or not depends entirely on the kind of damage and where it has occurred in the picture. If you have an oil painting of Lincoln Cathedral, let us say, and somebody has put his foot right through the middle of one of the towers, then no dealer is going to be very interested—unless the picture happens to be signed P. de Wint (Peter de Wint is a much-sought-after eighteenth-century artist who was very fond of Lincoln. He painted mainly in watercolour, but also did a few oils.) But if there is a small tear in one corner, then this can be repaired to look as good as new (or rather as good as old) at comparatively small expense—provided that the picture as a whole is worth it. This is really the important point. If the picture is going to be worth £100, it is clearly worth spending £10 or £15 on repairing minor damage. But to spend a similar sum on a worthless painting is merely throwing good money after bad. You must have a good idea of what you have found before making decisions of this kind, and you need expert advice before making up your mind.

**Frames**  Sad to say, picture frames are on the whole worthless if one thinks only in terms of direct sale. Almost the only exceptions (ignoring the possibility of finding a priceless Renaissance carved and gilded picture frame in your attic) are the maple frames which were extremely popular throughout the nineteenth century, and are now being sold again by dealers for their original purpose after some worthless print, perhaps, has been taken out. They come in all sizes, but they have certain common features. They are usually a speckled golden brown in colour, perfectly plain, and deep—often up to $1\frac{1}{2}$ inches all the way round the picture. The maple is almost invariably a veneer onto a frame of cheaper wood, but none the worse for that. It sometimes happens that one finds complete sets of matching frames of this kind, and these fetch a premium price. Our earlier remarks about condition apply here too, because it is quite common for

75

some of the veneer to have been split from the front of the frame.

Eighteenth- and nineteenth-century gilded frames of all sizes are also wanted. But there is one very common type of partially gilded frame which is almost certainly modern. This is known as the 'Hogarth' frame, and it is usually made up of a thin black moulded frame with a gilded strip, often patterned, both inside and outside the black.

Modern picture framing is horribly expensive, as anybody who has taken a picture to his local picture framer in recent years will have discovered. We rebelled against this a few years ago and taught ourselves to frame pictures at home. We had a lot of pictures and prints that we wanted to hang, but which were unframed; and a lot of framed odds and ends, mostly prints, which we never wanted to see again. Unfortunately it is one of the facts of life that an old frame never fits another picture, so that we either had to make new mounts (not too difficult) or do surgical operations on the frames themselves (very difficult until you get the hang of it). But anyone who is good with his hands (we started without this advantage) can learn to frame pictures without too many awful experiences, and if you have the same problems as we have, it is very well worth doing. An essential aid is a little book called *Picture Framing for Beginners* by Prudence Nutall (Studio Vista, 1968) which will tell you exactly what to buy in the way of the few tools and other materials you will need. So a pile of old frames, or framed rubbish which you do not want, can be a treasure by saving you a considerable amount of money in picture-framing charges. But if you have a number of old but undistinguished frames, please do not throw them away or burn them. There are hundreds of amateur artists, some of them extremely competent, who cannot afford to have their pictures decently framed. You will see the evidence of this if you go to any amateur art show; quite a lot of good work, in frames that look as if they have been torn from tea-chests. The secretary of the local art society (address from your library) will be delighted to pass on unwanted frames to deserving members.

The Victorian era was remarkable for (among other things)

its emphasis on home hobbies and entertainment. Practically every small girl from a middle-class home received lessons in painting, music, embroidery or some other useful accomplishment; and in many cases the habit stuck throughout life. Only a small proportion had the talent to paint in oils and watercolours, because to achieve any sort of standard one requires an inborn gift which only a few people are lucky enough to possess. But Victorian ladies were noted for their perseverance, and many of those who found that their talents were too small to make worthwhile pictures turned to arts and crafts of a slightly different kind. They produced the most elaborate pictures made of sand, or seaweed, or pricked out with pins on paper, or burnt in wood with red hot pokers. All these, being absolutely typical products of Victorian diligence, are enjoying a boom among collectors of Victoriana.

**Sandpictures** These are made up simply by trailing different coloured sands on to a surface covered with glue. With these extremely basic tools, some most attractive work was done. The result was titled, glazed and framed. Subjects vary enormously; we have a small one which shows one of the chines (valleys) running down to the beach on the Isle of Wight, a favourite subject because of the naturally coloured sand found there.

**Seaweed pictures** These are made in much the same way, using as many different varieties of seaweed as the artist could lay hands on. Subjects are of course much more limited and usually consist of representations of bouquets of flowers.

**Pyrographs** This is a name made up to describe a picture produced by scorching the subject into wood (it was also known later as poker-work). Pyrographs were extremely popular during the nineteenth century. It is an awkward and clumsy way of creating a picture, and many of the results demonstrate this. Some examples are of much finer quality, however, and nearly all of them are attractive to dealers.

In the early part of this chapter we mentioned paintings on porcelain. We shall deal with this in more detail in the chapter on pottery and porcelain. To end the present chapter we should, however, mention paintings on *glass*.

**Glass paintings**  Paintings on glass were made primarily to hang on the walls of cottage sitting-rooms. Most of them are of mid-to-late-Victorian vintage, and the majority are so crude that they have a real rustic charm which is very appealing to the modern collector. They were painted in oil paint on the back of a sheet of glass which was then (as a rule) placed against another sheet of glass so that the painting became the jam in the sandwich. It was then framed, often quite nicely, with maple veneer frames of the kind we described earlier in the chapter. Subjects are nearly always vaguely romantic country scenes—a ruined castle by a river with woods all around, or a cottage in a woodland glade. The colours are coarse and garish, or cheap and cheerful, and the whole production shows only the most rudimentary idea of design and painting. Nevertheless, collectors love them and this means they are highly saleable.

# 7
# Prints

A print is a reproduction of an original work of art. All prints are, as the word says, printed—that is, what you see is imprinted in ink on paper (or very occasionally on cloth or some other material, but that need not concern us here). There are all sorts of words which are used in connection with prints, and if you are going to have any idea at all of what you have in your attic, you must know what at least some of the more important of these terms mean.

As we said in the chapter on paintings, one of the ways of telling a picture from a print is to look for printed words on the edge If there is printing there, of any kind, then it is a print and not a picture. Hanging on a wall in our house there is a highly-coloured framed representation of four of the victorious generals from the Boer War. In tiny letters at the bottom-left-hand corner there is the phrase 'Entered at Stationers Hall' and on the opposite side the word 'Copyright'. This immediately tells us that it is a print and not a painting; 'Entered at Stationers Hall' is another way of saying 'Patented' and limits the right of this particular print to be reproduced. With its excellent (but not photographic) likenesses of the four generals, and its handsome bright colours, it is a *chromo-lithograph* (see below).

There are several different kinds of print, named according to the process that was used to make the original design. Clues are in the small printing at the bottom, and it is worth taking a magnifying glass to see what is said there. If the original from which the print was made was a drawing, in pen-and-ink or in pencil, there will probably be the abbreviation 'del.', meaning 'drawn by', followed by a name. If the

79

original was a painting in oils or watercolour then the word will be 'pinx.' or 'pinxit' followed by the name of the painter. These are usually in the bottom-left-hand corner of the print; in the bottom right-hand corner will be found the name of the engraver after the abbreviation 'sculp.' or the word 'sculpsit' meaning 'he engraved it'. Sometimes the words 'fec.' or 'fecit' are used instead; this merely means 'he made it'.

We have not so far used the word 'engraved'. Prints are often called engravings, and for all practical purposes this is quite an accurate term. In order to produce a print, the picture or scene has to be engraved (in reverse) in some hard material and then given a coat of printers ink so that it will make an impression in ink when it is pressed to a piece of paper. It is the different ways of engraving the block, and the different materials of the block itself, which make the various kinds of print. We will go briefly through these block-making materials and techniques and you will no doubt recognize many old friends among them.

**Etchings**  Etchings are familiar because young ladies are warned against being taken by young men to see them. The block (or rather the plate in this case) for an etching is produced by the action of acid. The artist–engraver takes a sheet of copper covered with a thin film of wax. He draws his picture in the wax with a fine needle. The plate is then put into a bath of acid and where the copper has been exposed by the artist's needle, it is eaten away by the acid. The plate is taken out of the acid bath after a time, washed, and the result is the artist's design etched into the copper plate. If printer's ink is put on to this plate and then wiped off, the ink remains in the etched lines and will print direct on to paper.

Many artists did their own etching, among them such famous names as Dürer and Rembrandt. However, far more likely to be found in attics are etched prints by Rowlandson, famous for his caricatures of political and social life in the late eighteenth century; and by Cruikshank, another well-known English caricaturist. Canaletto too, whose scenes of Venice and London are much prized by English collectors, was an excellent etcher in his own right.

*Hand-made brass parrot cage*
*of about 1880.*

*Some games and toys of earlier generations*

*Nineteenth-century billheads*

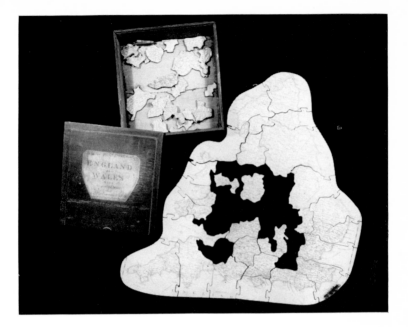

*An educational jigsaw puzzle of 1806*

*Great War souvenirs made from spent ammunition*

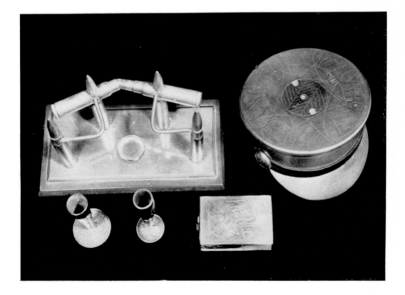

*A fine scrapbook of advertisements*

**Woodcuts** Wood engravings must not be confused with woodcuts; the two processes are the exact opposites of each other. For a woodcut, the cutter starts off with a slab of very hard wood (box wood is the traditional favourite) and after roughing out his design on the surface, he cuts away with a series of miniature chisels all those parts of the wood which he does *not* want to print in ink. At the end therefore he is left with a raised design, standing out from the main part of the block. This design can then be inked and printed direct on to paper.

Wood-cutting is probably the oldest method of making prints. It goes back certainly to the fifteenth century in this country.

Not many artists did their own woodcuts, because it is a much more difficult process than the comparatively simple business of drawing in wax which is all that is necessary for an etching. As a result, woodcuts were done, as a rule, by professional cutters working from the artist's original drawing or painting.

**Wood engraving** This is a comparatively young technique, and the process is exactly what it sounds like—the engraving of lines in wood in just the same way as line engravings (see below) are done on metal.

**Line engravings** Line engravings are produced by the straightforward process of cutting, with special hard chisels, lines in metal plates. Before about 1820, the metal used for line engraving was copper, which is comparatively soft. After 1820, steel plates were introduced (hence the term steel engraving) so that many more impressions could be taken from the same plate before it started to wear. Among the better-known engravings are those by Edward Goodall, who reproduced many of Gainsborough's paintings; the topographical scenes of William Finden (mid-nineteenth century); Robert Brandard's prints of Turner's work.

**Mezzotints** The mezzotint process, invented in 1641 by a German, does away with engraved lines and substitutes patterns of tiny dents in the basic plate. The plate is made of

81

copper, and the tool that makes the dents is called a rocker. There were many more stages after the creation of the dents in the copper plate, and the process was a complicated one. As a result, practically all mezzotints were done by professional engravers, after work by artists. Most of the best examples date from towards the end of the eighteenth century. Among highly-regarded mezzotint engravers are Edward Bell, George Keating, James McArdell, William Pether and Thomas Watson. A mezzotint engraving is very delicate, and there is a complete absence of heavy line. The whole effect is created by a pattern of fine tones of light and dark.

**Stipple engravings** These are the first cousins of etchings. The same basic equipment—a copper plate covered with wax —is used, but instead of cutting out lines in the wax, the engraver cuts out dots. This stippling (an artist uses the same term when he is painting in dots of colour) was particularly used for making prints from pencil drawings. The effect is soft and slightly misty, since there are no firm lines in the composition. Again, it was particularly popular in the second half of the eighteenth century. The best known stipple engraver (they were nearly all professionals working from artists' pictures) was Bartolozzi, whose most celebrated series is the 'Cries of London' after Wheatley. Thousands of copies —and a good many forgeries—have been produced; there are thirteen in the full set.

**Aquatints** An aquatint is a type of engraving which was intended to represent, as closely as possible, a watercolour. It was a complicated process which started from a simple etching, and was then followed by successive washes with acid. The process was rediscovered (after being abandoned at the end of the seventeenth century) in 1768, and was put to use by one or two well-known English artists for the reproduction of their work. Among them, Paul Sandby (a celebrated watercolour artist in his own right) engraved a most attractive series of aquatints called 'Twelve Views in North Wales'.

One of the best known names in aquatint engraving is Rudolph Ackermann, who produced a vast series of sporting and topographical aquatints, all of them engraved by specialists. Among other names to look for in aquatint prints are John Cleveley, who specialized in shipping; the brothers Daniel and Robert Havell, whose forte was stage coaches; and Thomas Sutherland, whose work includes coaching, military and sporting scenes.

**Lithographs** Lithography is the only process among the standard methods of producing prints that is not a form of engraving. Readers who remember any of their Greek from schooldays will recognize that the word lithograph is made up of two words indicating respectively stone and drawing. It is quite simply a drawing on stone; but the drawing instrument is a crayon of greasy material, and the stone is a special one which absorbs the grease. The final result, after the stone has been wetted with water and run through the inking press, is an extremely accurate reproduction of the artist's drawing. Lithography is one of the few processes (etching is another) that are sufficiently simple for artists to produce their work direct, without the intermediate work by a skilled engraver to make the plate. Very many artists, particularly in the last eighty years or so, have produced delightful lithographs. Among the well-known names are Whistler, Toulouse Lautrec, and many of the most celebrated artistic figures of the present century—Picasso, Chagall and Matisse, for example.

**Chromo-lithographs** Lithography was extended to allow colours to be printed at the same time, and chromo-lithographs were first produced in about 1830 and became important after the middle of the century. Before the invention of chromo-lithography, coloured prints could nonetheless be achieved, but they either had to be done by hand (many apparent 'watercolours' are in fact line engravings, coloured afterwards by hand) or by the equally laborious process of using coloured inks on the original blocks. This often necessitated a good deal of masking-off, or even complicated chemical processes, to achieve different colours in different parts of the print.

**Condition** Condition in prints, particularly where there is likely to be value in them, is as important as in any other branch of collecting. 'Foxing'—a spattering of brown spots—and general staining are very common among prints that have not been looked after.

**States** Equally important, where one is talking about collectable prints, is the 'state'. This is a technical term, and refers not so much to the print itself but to the condition of the plate from which the print was taken. Plates have a hard life. In order to get a good impression on the paper, the plate (or block, or stone, if we are talking about wood engravings or lithographs) is sent through the printer's press where it is subjected to very heavy pressure. After several journeys of this kind, the sharp edges of the engraved lines begin to become slightly blurred, and the resulting print loses a little of its crispness. This can get to the stage where the whole print is fuzzy; by then, the block should have been thrown away. So to a collector, a good 'state' is an early print from the plate (or block, or stone). Where really important artists (such as Rembrandt or Dürer among the Old Masters) are concerned, states are all-important in determining the price. In varying degrees, the same is true of any other good print.

One name is familiar to almost everyone when the subject of prints is being discussed—George Baxter. His great contribution to the art of prints was the invention of a process by which colours (any number of them) could be printed with great accuracy and fine detail. A separate block was used for every colour, and even for every shade of every colour; each block was separately printed to add its own individual colour to the whole. The process was introduced in 1835, and between that date and 1849 Baxter had a complete monopoly. After 1849, he granted licences to a few other artist–printers, among them Le Blond (who in 1867 actually acquired Baxter's own plates and blocks). Baxter's prints, which are always in colour, are much sought after by collectors, and will readily find good prices. Most eagerly collected is his series of pretty girls; next in popularity are his flower prints and landscapes. He produced about four hundred different prints in all; they are almost invariably signed.

**Stevengraphs** Of all the forgotten curiosities which you might come across in your search of the attic, the most valuable might well be a few Stevengraphs. These are little woven silk pictures in bright colours, made by Thomas Stevens in Coventry between 1879 (when the first Stevengraph pictures were produced) and 1940 (when the whole of Coventry was bombed flat). Until a few years ago, these pictures were no more than unconsidered trifles, and they could be bought in many cases for shillings rather than pounds. Today the situation is very different. Very rarely do you find one for less than £15, and the highest price paid for one so far is £520 (in 1969). The general feeling is that this rapid rise in price has practically reached its limit, and prices may well fall in the next period, except in the case of rare examples. However, for those who find them hidden away in the attics, the prices of practically any Stevengraphs will be extremely attractive.

They vary in size from about 13 inches by $7\frac{1}{2}$ inches to about 4 inches by $1\frac{1}{2}$ inches. They were woven in silk on a specially adapted Jacquard loom. A total of 180 different designs were produced by Stevens, and they vary tremendously in subject-matter and in value. Among the ones that are particularly sought after are those with American interest (scenes of Columbus departing for America and arriving there, or the signing of the Declaration of Independence) and other historical occasions (particularly ones associated with Coventry—Lady Godiva's ride is a particular example), as well as sporting scenes. The latter are particularly attractive. Among them are scenes of boat races, horse racing, a rugger match, and a couple of marvellous bicycle races, in one of which the riders are on penny-farthings. Among other subjects are royalty and personalities of the times, such as Gladstone, Kitchener; popular sporting heroes such as the jockey Fred Archer in his silks (variations in colour are known, and these can add to the value); and historical exhibitions.

All these subjects, and many others, were designed and woven with great delicacy—even the expression on people's faces can be clearly seen in the compass of the tiny picture.

There are two points of particular importance in deciding whether a particular Stevengraph is valuable or not. The first is that when they were originally sold, they were complete with a cardboard mount. This mount carries the title on the front, and should have Stevens's label on the back. The second point is that *condition* is all-important. Only those examples which still have their original bright colours will command the full price. And by the way, it is worth remembering that both Stevengraphs and watercolours suffer from the effects of sunlight. If you decide to hang a Stevengraph which has been discovered, put it in a shady corner or the brilliant colours will fade.

To whet your appetite, among the three most valuable Stevengraph pictures are *Leda and the Swan, The Spanish Bullfight* and *The Winter Gardens, Blackpool.*

Other firms, such as W. H. Grant, also made woven silk pictures. Their products are not, so far, in the same league as Stevengraphs, but within the next few years the value of these lesser-known competitors' efforts will certainly increase very considerably.

Both Stevens and his rivals also turned out large numbers of book-marks made in the same way as the pictures. Many were religious in subject—usually texts with embellishments—or the familiar Victorian exhortations to better thoughts or deeds. They fetch from about £3 upwards at the moment, but these too will rise in value.

# 8

# Musical instruments

Only if some earlier member of your family was a well-known performer might you find really valuable musical instruments in your house: and you are scarcely likely to be unaware of that. You should therefore resign yourself to the fact that the old violin you find in your attic is not a Stradivarius or an Amati and that the likelihood of finding one is about as great as finding a Rembrandt painting or a Caxton book.

In spite of that, there are quite a lot of things on the fringe of the musical world which you might easily find tucked away, and which are of interest and value. Some of them may be rather unexpected.

**Music covers**  The sheer volume of printed music that was turned out during the Victorian era is absolutely staggering. Almost every household had a piano. Almost every family had at least one member who could play it, and who could probably sing as well; and there was many a family that could muster a very respectable small choir from its own members. Musical evenings were as common as—and a great deal more fun than—cocktail parties are today. To cope with this demand, the music publishers turned out enormous quantities of ballads, both sentimental and heroic; comic songs, duets for four hands, harmonies for two voices; and all the other blueprints for home-made music.

The music itself is very rarely of much interest. But quite a lot of the numbers were bound in illustrated paper covers, and these in some cases are collectors' pieces. Most of them were lithographs (see Chapter 7), early ones having been coloured by hand, the later ones examples of the chromo-lithography process described earlier.

Music covers that are particularly sought after include: (a) those sung by well-known music-hall performers (who usually held the copyright) such as Vesta Tilley, George Robey, Harry Vance, Little Tich and so on; and (b) those drawn by one or two particular artists. Two artists especially are collected—Alfred Concanen and John Brandard. Concanen often did the complete job of drawing and making the lithograph of his designs; sometimes he did only the drawing, allowing other technicians to make the lithograph. This was usually quite evident from the details printed at the bottom of the cover; we have one music cover entitled 'The Adventures of Robinson Crusoe' written and sung ('with immense success') by Mr Harry Clifton. The cover consists of a series of highly coloured vignettes showing exciting episodes from the story of Robinson Crusoe. Printed in the bottom-left-hand corner are the words 'Alfred Concanen del. & lith.'—drawn and lithographed by Alfred Concanen.

John Brandard was, if anything, a better artist and a better lithographer than Concanen, but his work was done before the music-hall appeared on the scene. His music covers are therefore mainly concerned with opera and ballet.

Among other music-cover illustrators which collectors look for are Thomas Packer, Walton, Robert John Hamerton and Alfred Bryan. There are also a few examples still to be found of covers designed by such famous artistic figures as George Cruikshank and George Baxter (who was mentioned in Chapter 7 in connection with his unique contribution to colour printing).

It was quite common for a dozen or more songs, complete with their illustrated covers, to be bound together to form a book. This was a contemporary, not a later, habit and there is really no artistic reason why the bindings should not be taken to pieces and the original music covers separated again. Increasingly, music covers are being framed as attractive prints in their own right. The better-known artists are beginning to command quite high prices, and as the supply diminishes these prices will certainly advance.

**Gramophones** These have their own devoted band of collectors. Particularly required are the old wax-cylinder models, in which the record itself was not a flat disc but a cylinder about the size and shape of (we apologize, but it is the best comparison we can think of) the cardboard middle of a toilet roll. The needle and the small disc which contained the sound-producing box were applied direct to the side of the cylinder, and the sound came out of the small detachable horn on top. The whole apparatus was comparatively small, much the same size as a portable sewing machine.

The other type of early gramophone which is collected is the model immortalized by the 'His Master's Voice' advertisements—a square wooden box with a turntable on top, and a huge horn overshadowing everything.

Gramophone records themselves are keenly collected; some of them fetch high prices. Special wants are recordings by famous operatic stars of past years—Dame Nellie Melba, Chaliapin, Adelina Patti. There is also a passionate band of collectors who search for early 'blues' records. As with all serious branches of collecting, the subject is a specialized one and we are not qualified to give specialist advice on early records. But any pile of old records should be carefully gone through, and if necessary sorted into groups. Orchestral music is rarely of much interest to collectors; nor is dance music of later date than about 1930. Military band music is also of little interest—unless the band happens to be conducted by John Philip Sousa himself, in which case the record should be wrapped up with great care.

**Pianolas** The forerunner—and to some extent the contemporary—of the gramophone and its record was the pianola and its roll. This magnificent machine is enjoying a return to popularity, and pianolas in good (or even moderate) condition are readily saleable. It would be a strong man who managed to get a pianola up into the attic, but one has, to our personal knowledge, been turned out to make room for other furniture; we were fortunate enough to be given it. At first sight, a pianola is an ordinary upright piano. The differences are that in the centre of the upright panel facing the player there is a sliding door which, when opened, reveals

89

the mechanism for holding and turning the pianola roll; all
along the edge of the keyboard there is a narrow folding cover
concealing three or four levers; and above the normal pedals
there is another pair of large pedals which fold forward
from a clip and provide the motive power for the whole
performance.

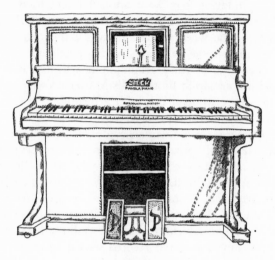

*Pianola*

The pianola will not work, of course, unless you have the
special rolls which were made to fit on the mechanism behind
the front panel. They are rolls of perforated paper, about
the thickness of one's wrist, and a standard length of 12
inches overall. How fat the roll is depends on how long the
piece may be; 'Selections from Wagner's *Parsifal*' is a good
deal more substantial than 'The Wedding of the Dragonfly—
Foxtrot', for example. Each roll, which is metal-ended,
should be in an individual box. Some makes of pianola
roll are more desirable than others. Particularly required by
pianola enthusiasts are rolls with the trade mark 'Duo-Art'.
These are semi-automatic, in that as well as the holes which
produce the actual notes, there are more holes along the side
of the roll which control the expression.

Pianola rolls were often 'cut' (if one can use that word)
by well-known artists, and the value to collectors is that in

90

many cases these rolls are the only record of how a particular artist played; for they had retired or died by the time that efficient sound recording appeared.

If you find a pianola in salvageable condition, ask a piano tuner to come and have a look at it. Piano tuning is, unhappily, a dying trade, and many of the dedicated and skilled men who do this work are approaching retirement. Experts like this will know about pianolas and will know what to do to put them in order, but in a few years' time it will be almost impossible to revive a damaged or neglected one except at enormous cost.

A word of warning too about pianola rolls. They are made of paper. The notes of the piano play when holes punched in the paper come opposite corresponding holes in the brass bar in the centre of the operating mechanism; the action of pedalling not only moves the roll on, but also pumps air through the holes to operate the hammers that strike the wires. The holes on the bar are very close together, and the correct functioning of a pianola depends entirely on the accuracy with which the holes in the roll are aligned with the holes on the bar. If the edges of the paper roll become torn, or crinkled and bent, it will not play properly and will be useless for ever. So it is worth taking great care of these rolls and making sure that they do not get damaged by careless handling. Quite ordinary rolls are changing hands for up to 50p each at the moment, and a pianola in good condition will certainly fetch £50. Both values will continue to increase.

**Polyphons** The pianola was really the earliest way of recording an individual interpretation. Before that, the most effective way of producing repeated performances of a piece of music by mechanical means was the polyphon. There were many different models, but they all operated on a variety of the musical-box principle; brass fingers, tuned to a fixed pitch, were lifted by tiny pegs on a cylinder or wheel, and as the peg passed the springy brass finger gave its note. Everybody knows what a musical box sounds like: they are still made today in vast quantities in Switzerland and Germany, mainly for the tourist trade. The early polyphons were much grander instruments, and because of their size they were capable of emitting a noise which could nearly knock you out of the room. We recently found in the attic of a country vicarage a polyphon of truly heroic proportions. It stood about 5 feet high and 3 feet wide. The 'record' was very like a modern record—except that it was made of brass, 2 feet in diameter, was covered with little projecting pegs, and was fitted in so that it revolved vertically instead of horizontally. The whole machine (which was at least eighty years old) was in full working order in spite of having been hidden away for a couple of generations, and was complete with a stock of about thirty brass discs. It is probably worth as many pounds as it is years old.

**Musical boxes**   These have already been mentioned, even though it was in rather a disparaging way. In the eighteenth and most of the nineteenth centuries, however, musical boxes were the most delightful works of art. Watchers of *Going for a Song* on BBC television will know the pretty singing bird which introduces the programme. This is typical of the workmanship of musical boxes and automata of the period. They all operate on clockwork mechanisms and some (particularly the eighteenth-century French ones) are extremely highly valued examples of the watchmaker's and jeweller's crafts. Musical boxes of this standard are unlikely to be found in attics, but it is very possible that humbler examples will be. It is not always easy to tell, at first sight, if what you have found is in fact a musical box. External clues will be found in the winding mechanism, which must always appear somewhere (it may be merely a keyhole) and the trip lever which starts it. In many cases the printed label which appears inside the lid or underneath the box gives details of the maker.

**Automata**   Automata do not, strictly speaking, fall within the category of musical items but they are so akin to musical boxes that this seems an appropriate place to include them. Clockwork mechanisms (which are in effect adult toys) have fascinated both craftsmen and patrons for centuries. Among the most interesting to modern collectors are the large wall-

*French nineteenth-century automaton*

mounted scenes contained in a glass case, perhaps 4 feet square, parts of which burst into action when a clockwork motor is set in motion by pressing a lever, or even by the insertion of a penny. Soldiers march across battlements, ships rock on a stormy sea, fish swim through murky depths as mermaids wave their arms. These mechanical scenes are close relatives of the prewar amusement arcade penny-in-the-slot machines (most of which concentrated on such macabre events as murderers being hanged) and we have seen them on sale in antique shops at prices which would buy quite a reasonable second-hand car.

# 9
# China

We never stop being amazed at the number of houses we find (and these are houses of all kinds, from suburban semis to large country mansions) in which all the interesting and potentially valuable china is knocking about in the attic or the kitchen, while the display cabinets or the Sunday parlour are full of modern rubbish. It is easy to be critical, of course. In some cases this may be a deliberate policy; but we rather doubt it. One titled lady that we know was horrified to find when she had an insurance valuation done that the little dish that she used for pins on her dressing table was worth more than a thousand pounds.

People who are not collectors find, in our experience, that the idea of getting to grips with identifying the china in their own houses is a frightening one, because of the sheer size of the project. 'How on earth,' they say, 'can I possibly learn if something is good or bad, if it is Wedgwood or Meissen?' Of course the finer points are beyond the amateur, and the dealers have built up their detailed and specialized knowledge through years of experience, and particularly through handling hundreds and thousands of examples. But it is knowing where to start which seems to be the biggest stumbling block, so—start here.

At the very beginning, we have to know what we mean when we use certain basic words. This chapter is headed 'China'. It really ought to be headed 'China and pottery' for this reason: *pottery* is simply baked clay. It may have all sorts of things done to it in the way of painted decorations, or shiny glaze, but underneath it is just clay, modelled by hand or on a machine, and baked in an oven. *China* is another word for *porcelain*, and it is a mixture of special clays and stones ground together, modelled and baked in a much hotter oven than is needed for pottery. Porcelain is much thinner and finer, and generally more delicate than pottery.

Pottery goes back to the beginning of civilization, but porcelain (or china) was originally invented by the Chinese centuries ago; the secret of making it was discovered in Europe in only 1708.

So how do you tell the difference between pottery and porcelain? It is extremely easy. There is no need to look at the marks, or to stroke it, or to tap it with your fingernail and look wise—all you need is a torch. Press the button of the torch, put the end of it against the cup, plate, jug or whatever it may be. If you can see a glow when you look from the other side of it, then it is porcelain. If you can't, it is pottery. There is nothing more difficult to it than that.

People often get the idea that pottery is the poor relation of porcelain, and that pottery can never be valuable while porcelain always is (this probably explains the horrid, garish, machine-made pieces of modern porcelain which we so often see exhibited proudly in display cabinets). It is, of course, quite untrue. There is valuable pottery and worthless porcelain, just as there is worthless pottery and valuable porcelain. It all depends when it was made, who made it and what it is.

Having decided that something you have found in the attic is porcelain because it is translucent, or pottery because it isn't, the problem of identification has immediately been cut in half. The next thing to do is to look on the bottom and see if there are any *marks*. Most books about antiques become very cautious at this stage. They will say that marks are often forged, and that they should be used for identifying porcelain (in particular) only as a last resort, and that you should learn to be able to recognize such things as hard and soft paste, glaze, style and all the professional pointers to date and factory of origin before relying on the marks. This is perfectly true if you are trying to buy something in a shop: before you part with your money you must make absolutely certain of what you are buying.

But you do not need this expertise when you are trying to decide if something you have found in your attic is worth getting excited about. More than that, in buying from a shop you never quite know where your purchase has come from; whereas anything you find in your attic bears a very strong likelihood that it is exactly what it seems to be. So we are not, in these circumstances, concerned about the subtleties of identification.

We may find no marks at all on the bottom—not every pottery or porcelain manufacturer marked his products. If there are marks, they may be one (or more, or all) of the following kinds: *factory* marks, *pattern* marks or a *registration* mark. Let us first look at the identification of various kinds of pottery.

**Pottery**  Factory marks tell you where the piece was made. For example, if your torch test has established that what you have found in your attic is a piece of pottery, it might have one of the following factory marks on the bottom:

*Wedgwood,* the most famous name in English pottery. Marked pieces start from about 1759, and the most common mark is simply the word 'Wedgwood' impressed in the pottery.

*Spode* (who also made china). The printed word 'SPODE' was used from about 1805 on the very popular printed earthenware products.

*Mason's* (usually followed by 'Patent Ironstone China' printed below a crown). This factory made very colourful wares in a special hard and heavy pottery. It was (and is) popular simply for its decorative qualities.

*Doulton,* both printed and impressed marks were used. 'Royal Doulton' was used from 1920.

*Pattern* marks are of little interest to us as attic treasure-hunters. They are usually small figures painted somewhere on the bottom. They were mainly for the use of the factory itself in identifying its own wares.

The *registration* mark is important, because we can get a fairly accurate idea of the date of the piece from the information contained in the mark itself. As you will see from the illustration, the registration mark was a lozenge-shaped design; it was usually printed or embossed in the base of a piece; it acted as a form of patent. It was used only between 1842 and 1883, and it is now regarded by collectors as almost conclusive proof of genuine Victorian products. The

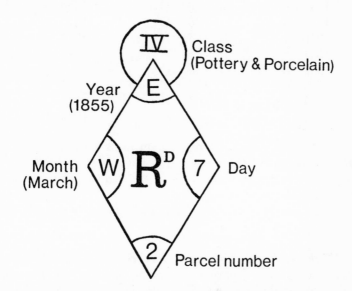

*Pottery or porcelain registration mark for 7 March 1855*

Americans in particular are avidly collecting anything that bears the Victorian registration mark. The mark shows the day, the month and the year of the registration of the design at the British Patent Office. The information is contained in the letters and numbers marked in the corners of the lozenge. The roman figure at the top, outside the lozenge, shows the class of ware; for example, ceramics (the general term for all pottery and porcelain) was Class IV. The letter immediately below this, in the top corner of the lozenge, shows the year of registration (if the piece was recorded between 1842 and 1867. For pieces entered between 1868 and 1883, the letter

97

G

is in the right-hand corner). The letters, with the dates to which they refer, are as follows:

| | | | | | |
|---|---|---|---|---|---|
| 1842 | X | 1856 | L | 1870 | C |
| 1843 | H | 1857 | K | 1871 | A |
| 1844 | C | 1858 | B | 1872 | I |
| 1845 | A | 1859 | M | 1873 | F |
| 1846 | I | 1860 | Z | 1874 | U |
| 1847 | F | 1861 | R | 1875 | S |
| 1848 | U | 1862 | O | 1876 | V |
| 1849 | S | 1863 | G | 1877 | P |
| 1850 | V | 1864 | N | 1878 | D |
| 1851 | P | 1865 | W | 1879 | Y |
| 1852 | D | 1866 | Q | 1880 | J |
| 1853 | Y | 1867 | T | 1881 | E |
| 1954 | J | 1868 | X | 1882 | L |
| 1855 | E | 1869 | H | 1883 | K |

So if your piece has a registration mark showing an E in the top corner of the lozenge, you know that the piece was registered in 1855; if the E is in the right-hand corner, it was registered in 1881.

What are the pieces most likely to be found in an attic, so far as pottery is concerned?

*Wash-stand sets* These are very common attic-dwellers. There are also a surprising number of houses where they are still used, partly because such a lot of houses still do not have running water, and partly because many older people still prefer to use them.

They usually consist of a large jug and basin, with a covered slop pail. You may think that such unromantic pieces of domestic china are unlikely to appeal to anybody, but this is not at all true. If the pieces bear the Victorian registration mark mentioned above, they are saleable for that reason alone. If they bear the Wedgwood mark, this is a stamp of quality in itself. If they are marked 'Wemyss'—well, this requires special mention.

The Wemyss pottery was one of the few that operated in the nineteenth century in Scotland. All its products are very much collected, and luckily they are easily recognizable.

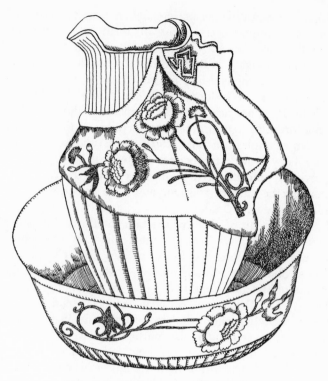

*Edwardian bedroom washbasin and jug*

Firstly, the ware is almost invariably marked with the word 'Wemyss' either impressed or painted (usually in green) on the bottom of the ware. Secondly, the patterns are un-mistakeable—nearly always fruit or flowers; huge blowsy roses, tulips, strawberries, cherries; very occasionally bees. We know one simply beautiful Wemyss wash-stand set which is at this moment sitting in an attic; it would take somebody on a very comfortable fortnight's holiday in the sun if it were sold.

*Staffordshire figures* So far as value is concerned, Staffordshire portrait figures are among the most important things that one is likely to find, hidden away or otherwise disregarded, in the house.

Enormous quantities of pottery figures were turned out by dozens of manufacturers, most of them in Staffordshire, during the Victorian era. They were the last in a long tradition of figure-making in Staffordshire. We shall not deal with these earlier examples, since figures made by master potters such as Astbury, Whieldon, the Wood family, the Sherratts and Felix Pratt are now extremely expensive. But the Victorian Staffordshire figures are rising in price all the time, and the rarer examples are now worth sums running into three figures. They provide the perfect example of how some kinds of previously unconsidered 'junk' have, since the war, struck a chord in the modern collector and have consequently risen steadily in value.

In the hey-day of their production, Staffordshire portrait figures decorated every cottage mantelpiece in the country. They were never intended to be anything but cheap, mass-produced objects for a totally unsophisticated public. It is their very unsophistication that makes the appeal to the modern collector. The Victorian country cottager tended to be fervently patriotic, sentimental, non-Conformist in his religion and a great lover of animals—particularly dogs. Even if he could read he scarcely ever did, and he relied for his news on gossip passed by word of mouth, and for his entertainment on things of the country (and, very occasionally, a live presentation such as a cock-fight). The Staffordshire figures deliberately appealed to all these feelings—these days we would probably say that the potters had done good market research—and so the subjects of the figures fall into a few well-defined groups. The biggest group was royalty: Queen Victoria was very co-operative in producing a whole host of princes and princesses (four of one and five of the other) who then went on to keep themselves in the public eye by marrying and having children of their own. Thousands of figures of Queen Victoria herself were made, some standing beside Prince Albert with her children, some on horseback, some sitting on a seat or a throne. He too was modelled in many different poses. Models of their children, and the (mostly foreign) princes and princesses that they married, include the Prince of Wales, Princess Victoria, Prince Frederick William of Prussia, Princess Alice, Prince Louis of Hesse,

*Staffordshire figure: The Prince of Wales*

Prince Alfred, the Duke of Connaught, Princess Louise and
the Marquis of Lorne, and the Duke of Cambridge (Queen
Victoria's uncle).

All sorts of military figures were made, because
the Staffordshire figures also acted as newspaper headlines.
The Crimean War of 1854–6 produced a whole crop of
military and naval heroes (including a few drawn from our
allies Turkey, France and Sardinia). Among the several dozen
notable personages that were modelled as figures, the best
known are Lord Raglan, who commanded the British Army

101

in the Crimea (and who incidentally gave his name to the Raglan sleeve) and Florence Nightingale, who needs no introduction.

Between the Crimean War and the Boer War of 1899–1902, there was a whole host of minor skirmishes, mainly on the frontiers of Africa and India, and two more serious affairs with the Indian Mutiny (1857–9) and the Egyptian and Sudanese wars of 1892–8. A famous personage from the Indian Mutiny who was modelled in pottery was not a general, nor even a man, but 'Highland Jessie'. She was the wife of a Corporal Brown, and was besieged with her husband and his regiment in Lucknow in 1857. When all seemed lost during the siege, she put new heart into the garrison by screaming that she could hear the sound of the pipes leading the rescue column. This is said to be the origin of the fine tune 'The Campbells are Coming'.

Many religious figures (nearly all of them non-Conformists as we have explained) were made, including such famous personalities as General Booth, founder of the Salvation Army, and the celebrated pair of revivalist preachers from America, Moody and Sankey.

Among the most desirable of the Staffordshire portrait figures from the Victorian era are the contemporary villains—particularly the murderers. It was here that Staffordshire figures took the place of newspapers. The horrible episode known as the Murder in the Red Barn was faithfully recorded in pottery (it actually happened in 1828) with the figures of the murderer William Corder and his victim Maria Marten, and the grisly Red Barn itself. Palmer the Poisoner is another celebrated murderer who was commemorated in this way.

Equally collected are the figures, many of them extremely rare, of Victorian sportsmen. These include boxers such as Heenan and Sayers, who fought a marathon bare-fisted championship fight in 1860; and Tom Cribb, champion of England from 1809 to 1824. Cricketers are the most eagerly collected of all figures, and include Fuller Pilch, Thomas Box and Fred Lilywhite. There is at least one jockey, Fred Archer, made in about 1875; and even a couple of fast greyhounds called Master MacGrath and Pretender.

Many politicians were made, including the Duke of Wellington, Daniel O'Connell, Sir Robert Peel and Mr Gladstone (Mrs Gladstone was modelled too). There are folk-heroes like Grace Darling, notabilities such as Mrs Amelia Bloomer, who first wore the strange garments named after her; flamboyant characters like the Lionslayer (that is what the figure is called) Roualeyn George Gordon-Cuming, a highly successful big-game hunter.

*Staffordshire figure: The Lionslayer*

The variety of Staffordshire figures is enormous. The collector today is looking mainly for those figures which have the person's name marked on the base. The figures stand about 9–12 inches high on average, and the titles appear in raised letters, or sometimes in black or gold script. Untitled figures are generally much less valuable than the titled ones; and even among the titled ones, it is the representations of contemporary personalities (such as we have described above) which collectors are searching for. The range is so wide, and the subject such a fascinating one, that anybody who has one or more titled figures in the attic (or perhaps still on the mantelpiece) should consult either our own little book *Discovering Staffordshire Figures* (Shire Publications, 1969) or the more comprehensive *Staffordshire Figures of the Victorian Age* by Thomas Balston (Faber & Faber, 1958).

We have not so far mentioned the type of Staffordshire figure which is probably better known than any other—the spaniel dog. Several different models were made, but the commonest are the brown and white (occasionally black and white) animals about 7 inches in height, sitting down with their heads turned sideways. They were almost invariably made in pairs. Bigger and smaller models in similar positions were also made. These spaniels are the most common of the Staffordshire dogs, but there are also greyhounds (sometimes sitting and sometimes lying on cushions, and occasionally holding a hare in their mouths) and cats.

As always, the earlier examples tend to be more valuable than the later ones, although with Staffordshire figures the rarity and interest of the personality itself is often the more important factor. Named personalities can easily be dated by reference to one of the books mentioned above (biographies from the library are not much use in this case) and as a general indication to date, the more colour there is on the figure the earlier it is. Late figures (1870 onwards) were very sketchily decorated, often being reduced to white with a few black lines, a bit of gilding and perhaps a touch of pink on the cheeks.

As a guide to values, the following prices were realized at a sale held in 1969 at Christie's:

Florence Nightingale with a wounded officer
   (Crimean War, 1855)          28 guineas
Garibaldi (Italian War of Independence)    38 guineas
Prince Alfred in naval dress            63 guineas

| | |
|---|---|
| Princess Louise and her husband the Marquis of Lorne | 90 guineas the pair |
| Mrs Bloomer | 100 guineas |
| Heenan and Sayer, the boxers | 120 guineas |

Because of this kind of value, a great many Staffordshire figures have been forged in modern times. However, as we have already said this is comparatively unimportant: your own unknown treasures are unlikely to be modern copies.

Now for a few more individual items in pottery that dealers and collectors are looking for.

*Chamberpot made by the Belleek Factory, showing Gladstone's head*

*Chamberpots* (More commonly known as jerries.) Unexpected though it may be, 'handsome' and 'interesting' (dealer's terms) jerries are popular items among collectors, not only for their handsomeness or their interest but as plant pots too. Of course they vary greatly in quality and design, and only rather special ones will put a gleam in a collector's eye. Any example with a Victorian registration mark is, of course, a certain success as we have already mentioned. As an example of a really interesting one, we found some years ago on a junk stall a small jerry made by the firm of Belleek, an Irish pottery. Products of the Belleek factory are collected in themselves, but what made the jerry an item of major interest was that inside, on the bottom, there was a painting of Gladstone's head. This was of course a political joke of the most earthy kind, and collectors of political material have begged us to sell it to them at prices which makes its original cost on the junk stall—25p—ridiculous. This particular item is, so far as our experience goes, unique; but there are many other examples of particular forms of decoration which will be saleable.

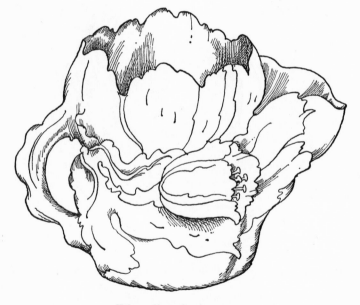

*Edwardian shaving mug*

*Toiletware* Less controversial are shaving mugs. These items of toiletware, essential to every man before the invention of brushless shaving, always remind us of pot-bellied pelicans. All are saleable, but the ones with attractive or interesting decorations, such as the glowing pink-lustre-decorated example in our own collection, will fetch the better prices.

*Dressing-table sets* They occupied every Victorian and Edwardian woman's dressing table, and are not on the whole very easy to sell unless there is something very special about them. There are just too many that have come on to the market, and a great many of them are poor, mass-produced stuff.

*Victorian footbaths* These, on the other hand, usually made of a particularly hard and heavy form of pottery called stoneware, are much in demand. They are just enormous, flat-bottomed, straight-sided bowls in which tired feet could be plunged into one of the solutions (hot water and mustard was a favourite) which the Victorians thought would do them good.

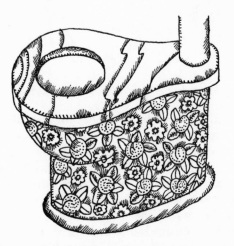

*Blue and white transfer-printed lavatory bowl*

*Transfer-printed ware* There is one particular kind of toiletware which is in great demand by collectors and interior decorators. This is the most attractive transfer-printed ware, the decorations usually being in blue on white and consisting of close-packed masses of foliage, from which matching sets of water-closet and wash-basin were made. Water-closets came into general use in only about 1870; these transfer-printed pottery sets were some of the earliest to be fixed into houses to celebrate the event. They may therefore still be found *in situ,* and possibly still in use. Anyone who still has such a set in operation may well find the sale of it would go a considerable way towards paying for a brand-new modern set—which will certainly be more efficient even if it is not as attractive.

*Meat dish from Victorian dinner service*

*Plates* If they are individual ones (or even if they are in sets), plates are of little value unless there is something special about them—outstanding patterns, particular makers or the Victorian registration mark. The only exceptions are the huge Victorian and Edwardian meat dishes which in medieval days would have been called chargers. They often have, moulded at the end of the dish, a well for the gravy with little herring-bone channels to take it there. These meat dishes, sometimes as much as 3 feet long, are big enough to form a centrepiece for a scheme of decoration.

*Complete dinner sets* Complete sets in pottery, including all the necessary items such as plates, tureens, dishes, meat dishes and gravy boats, can be of considerable value if they are (a) large enough, (b) complete and (c) of attractive design. These are not as a rule bought by collectors, but by families who want to use them for their original purpose. We often eat from a most decorative set made by Spode in about 1840, which has representations of Aesop's Fables printed in pale mossy green on a white background. When it is not in use, this set is displayed on a white-painted kitchen dresser, and very handsome it looks. We paid £25 a year ago and think it was extremely cheap at that price.

This Aesop's Fables set is an example of a pattern which is saleable. Another is the famous willow pattern, of which there are several different varieties according to the pottery that made the set. Wedgwood first produced wares bearing the willow pattern in 1795, but other potteries (including Spode) also used it. If you have a Wedgwood willow pattern set, or even a single plate, you will find that the apple tree has got thirty-four apples on it. Some other patterns have thirty-two apples; one factory, Rockingham (which made porcelain rather than pottery), removed the apple tree altogether.

*Flower vases* There are few things as attractive to arrange flowers in as an old Victorian pottery flower vase. More and more people are realizing this, and attractive examples, particularly of the very large and the very small sizes, are wanted.

We have not mentioned any really early pottery in this section. This is not because early pottery has no value—far from it; some early pottery, English or foreign, is extremely valuable —but because the likelihood of finding any hidden away is extremely small. If you find a pot (which is a term which covers anything made of pottery, from plates to figures) which you have reason to believe is really old, then you should take it straight to your local museum and ask their advice. The subject is too specialized to be dealt with in a book of this kind.

Do not, however, be too hopeful if you find a *Toby jug*. This enormously popular pattern has been copied and reproduced and copied again for the last hundred years or more, and the chances of finding a valuable original model are remote in the extreme. The phrase 'Toby jug' covers a

*Toby jug,* circa *1790*

large range of small jugs formed into the likenesses of various characters, only one of which was the celebrated Toby Philpot. You get sailors, pirates, fiddlers, Punch and Judys, John Bull (and also a few generals from the First World War—and those *are* of value).

*Puzzle jug*
110

Two other classes of miscellaneous pottery should be mentioned before we move on to porcelain. *Puzzle jugs* were a popular form of novelty in Victorian days. They go back, in fact, much earlier than that but most of the examples one sees in antique shops are Victorian. The 'puzzle' about a puzzle jug was how to get the contents out without soaking yourself and the surroundings; for the top half of the jug is made up of a pottery lattice work—rather like a coarse net—which appears to make it quite impossible to get the contents out without a disaster. The secret (as a rule) is that there is a connection between the bottom of the jug and the top rim, via the hollow handle. By putting your fingers over one or two secret holes, you could suck at one of the projecting spouts round the top rim, and the contents of the jug would come from the bottom up the handle. Pottery puzzle jugs are very popular at the moment.

*Early nineteenth-century frog mug*

Equally popular are *frog mugs,* another rather heavy-handed Victorian joke. The large pottery mug is found to have, inside it at the bottom, a large life-like pottery frog, painted in full and accurate colours. The joke here was to watch the drinker's face when he had lowered his beer sufficiently to see the frog's face sticking out of it. Roars of earthy laughter—and nowadays a ready sale.

**Porcelain** We shall not spend as long on porcelain as we have on pottery, simply because porcelain is not, as a rule,

111

consigned to the attic. But many readers will use this book to identify possessions elsewhere in the house, and for that reason we are including a brief account of the main types and makes of porcelain, and a few words on each to help identification.

The best known *German* porcelain is Meissen. This is where the first European porcelain was made in 1708. The Meissen factory was situated near the town of *Dresden* (now in Eastern Germany) and for this reason Meissen and Dresden are often used equally to describe the products of the factory. Collectors tend to use 'Meissen' for the earlier, more valuable porcelain, and 'Dresden' for the later (including modern) ware.

The Meissen mark is a pair of crossed swords, nearly always in blue. Unfortunately this mark was copied by dozens of porcelain factories all over Europe, and it is therefore an expert's job to decide whether a particular piece carrying this mark is in fact a product of the Meissen factory or not.

Other well-known German porcelain factories are Nymphenburg (mark—two superimposed triangles), Höchst (a wheel with four or six spokes), Frankenthal and Berlin (an eagle and/or the letters KPM).

Of all the *French* porcelain factories, Sèvres is the best known. Its decoration is outstanding, and the Sèvres factory produced some of the loveliest and most costly porcelain ever seen. The most common mark is two flowing letter 'L's crossed together. There is also a useful pointer as to date, in that between 1753 and 1793 the factory made a habit of marking its wares with a letter indicating the year (rather in the same way as the Victorian registration mark already mentioned). Other famous French factories are Vincennes (forerunner of Sèvres), Saint-Cloud, and Chantilly (mark— a hunting horn).

If you have good porcelain in your house, it is most likely to be *English*. Many of the English factories are still in operation under the same name, and therefore it is again a task for the expert to give an accurate identification and date. The earliest, and most valuable, English porcelain was made by the *Bow* and *Chelsea* factories. Both these were of course in London, and they started work in 1740 and 1750 respectively.

112

Neither lasted very long. The Bow factory rarely used a mark; Chelsea used as a rule an anchor mark, red for its early ware, gold for the later products.

*Worcester*, still going strong in its parent city, was also founded more than two hundred years ago. Its most usual mark is a blue crescent but other marks including various combinations of the letters B, F and B were also used. From 1891, the words 'Royal Worcester England' were common.

*Worcester mark*

*Derby mark*

*Derby*, which took over the Chelsea factory when it failed, used a red D as its main mark. Products after about 1770 had a crown added over the D; this is the famous Crown Derby. Crown Derby porcelain is often less valuable than the earlier uncrowned Derby ware.

*Swansea* and *Nantgarw* were two factories in Wales which were founded by one of the most famous figures in English porcelain, William Billingsley. The products of these two factories are very valuable; the marks are simply 'Swansea' or 'Nantgarw' pressed into the paste or painted on.

*Spode* and *Copeland* are (for general purposes) the same factory. It made porcelain as well as pottery, and the factory is still in action and highly regarded by collectors of modern porcelain. An exhibition of Spode wares was held in London in 1970 to mark the factory's bicentenary.

There is one very useful pointer to dates on Victorian porcelain (and pottery). If the word 'England' appears as part of the mark on the bottom of any piece, then it automatically means that the piece was made after 1891.

113

H

You will appreciate that it is quite impossible for us to do more than give the very briefest outline of this enormous subject: we ourselves have a reference shelf of nearly fifty books about pottery and porcelain alone. But we can at least point our readers' noses in the right direction. The next thing to do is to get hold of a copy of the *Encyclopaedia of British Pottery and Porcelain Marks* by Geoffrey Godden (Barrie & Jenkins, 1964). This fascinating volume is not something that the casual attic hunter will want to buy—it costs £8. But it is absolutely invaluable for anybody who is concerned in more than a general way with British pottery and porcelain. If you want to know the date of, and more about, almost any piece of old or modern pottery or porcelain that you may come across, this volume will tell you (provided that your attic treasure has a legible mark on it).

Finally, in this quick excursion into the fascinating world of the porcelain collector, we will mention two particular types of ware which are much collected. They are at opposite ends of the financial scale.

The first is the *ship bowl*. Some of the English factories, notably the small one at Liverpool, produced during the late eighteenth and early nineteenth centuries some large and most

*Ship bowl from Liverpool factory*

attractive bowls, up to 2 feet across, decorated with 'portraits' of ships together with details of them (and often of their owner or captain too). These ship bowls were almost invariably commissioned pieces—possibly the owner ordered from the Liverpool factory a bowl bearing the picture of his ship, and used it for advertising purposes (in his shipping office) or simply to remind himself of his proud vessel. We have mentioned elsewhere how the English have always been particularly fond of anything to do with the sea, and that this extends equally to collectors and what they collect. The result is that these late-Georgian and Victorian ship bowls command very high prices.

*Crested china,* including the particularly saleable *Goss,* has already been mentioned in Chapter 4. We would merely repeat at this point that the examples of crested china which fetch good prices are (a) anything made by W. H. Goss, and so marked; (b) anything obviously to do with the Great War, particularly such things as aeroplanes, balloons, 'Keep the Home Fires Burning' ranges, and submarines: (c) items of *contemporary* (that is between about 1910 and 1925) period interest such as bathing beauties emerging from beach bathing machines, open charabancs or trams, horn gramophones or a man in headphones sitting at a crystal wireless receiver; and (d) houses and cottages. At the moment the only ones of these latter that fetch really high prices are the ones by W. H. Goss, but there is no doubt that the similar models made by other manufacturers (such as Willow Art) will eventually reach prices not far below.

The range of patterns produced in the form of crested souvenirs is absolutely staggering. We have been keeping a close eye on this particular market during the last ten years, and almost every month we come across some example that we have never seen before. In fact, 98 per cent of the products are almost valueless, as they were when they were first made. The other 2 per cent are well worth having. The more general type of antique dealer will buy collections (the larger the better) including both types.

# I0

# Metals

There are probably more misunderstandings and disappointments caused by metal antiques—or rather by pieces *thought* to be antique—than by all the rest put together. For the purposes of this chapter, 'metal' includes silver, copper and brass, pewter and—perhaps surprisingly in connection with antiques—cast iron.

**Silver** We are not going to tell you all about antique silver in this book. There is a whole range of works, from the general to the specialized, which you will find at your public library. What we can do is to give you a pretty accurate idea as to whether what you have is really silver or not. The prices paid for good English silver, particularly of the Georgian period, has been one of the wonders of the antique world during the course of the last ten years. They reached such a great height, in fact, that about a year ago the prices seemed to be levelling off, and in some cases even starting to come down. But there is now an indication that the prices are on the way up again—all of which goes to show that if you have some early silver tucked away, and you want to realize its value, the time is very ripe.

Remember first of all that silver is silver-coloured only if it is clean. Pieces that have been put away for a long time, particularly in a damp atmosphere, may have become almost black. This does not mean they are damaged by the tarnishing—it is a very thin film, easily removable with the proper treatment (see below).

116

From the collector's point of view, one of the very best things about silver is that it can, with the rarest exceptions, be dated accurately and beyond any doubt. All you have to do is to be able to read the marks, and this is really quite easy. Every piece of English silver, except very small items, has been stamped with marks ever since 1544. As a rule these marks, which were stamped permanently into the metal with a die, are to be found in some inconspicuous place—very often underneath—but this is not always true; particularly in the earlier pieces (Elizabethan and Stuart) they seemed to take a delight in putting the marks in the most conspicuous place they could find. For the last two hundred years or so, marks have been small—about the size of a grape pip—but as there are usually four or five of them all in a row, they are quite easy to find.

Now, what are these marks? They may be in any order, but the ones which must appear are:

*The sterling mark* This shows that the metal contains at least the minimum amount of pure silver. This mark is a 'lion passant'—the side view of a complete lion. There was also a short period (between 1697 and 1719) when a higher standard was enforced and the lion was replaced by a seated figure of Britannia.

*The assay mark* This mark shows the town where the piece was tested. Only certain cities had the right to maintain an Assay Office, and each city had a different mark. The most important assay marks are: (a) The *leopard's head* of *London*. Until 1820, the leopard's head had a crown, but in 1820 it was done away with; (b) the *anchor* of *Birmingham,* (c) the *three castles* of *Edinburgh,* (d) the *harp* of *Dublin*.

There were several other Assay Offices, including Glasgow, Exeter, Chester, Sheffield, Norwich and York; each one had its own distinctive symbol. In modern times the number of Assay Offices has been reduced, and some of the ones mentioned above no longer exist.

*The date letter* From the point of view of deciding how old the piece is, this is the most important mark. It is also

117

the one that people find most difficult to decipher, and there is some justification for this. When the Goldsmiths decided to have a mark to identify the year of manufacture, instead of saying 'Let us use the last two figures of the date, so that for example 23 will mean 1623 or 1723 or 1823 or 1923', they said 'Let us use the letters of the alphabet'. As a further complication, they also decided to leave out seven of them. The result was that they had to find a way of distinguishing between the same letter coming round every twenty years. To

*Examples of letter styles used in hall-marking*

achieve this they had to alter the style of the letter and the shape of the shield in which it lies. So it comes about that on London-marked silver the date letter for 1796 is a plain capital A in a small shield, which is pointed at the bottom. You will find the letter A is used again for the date letter to indicate the year 1916, but although the shield is the same shape, the letter is a small gothic 'a'.

It is quite impossible for anybody, even an expert, to carry in his head all these letters and styles. If you are a regular watcher of *Going for a Song* on television, you will know that

Arthur Negus can usually date a marked piece of silver with great accuracy. This is not the result of magic, nor even a photographic memory. He carries in his mind one letter related to one year—let us say 'p' for 1750. With his experience, and with the clues he gets from the other marks (such as the sovereign's head mentioned below), he has a reasonably good idea as to the period of the piece to within, say, twenty-five years. It is then just a matter of reading the date letter, and counting. It should be noted, however, that the different Assay Offices used different sequences, so that 'p' means 1750 only on silver with the leopard's head of London on it.

*The sovereign's head* Between 1784 and 1890, every piece of English silver was marked, in addition to the other marks already mentioned, with the head of the ruling sovereign, to show that duty had been paid. The sovereigns during this period were George III, George IV, William IV and Queen Victoria. Unless the marks have been badly worn away by wear, one can usually recognize which sovereign it is—and of course Queen Victoria, the only female, is unmistakable.

*Maker's mark* Makers were required, by the rules of their livery company, to mark their products; each maker used another die which showed either his initials or a symbol of some kind. Among the most famous of initials are PS for Paul Storr, and HB for Hester Bateman.

If you have any silver in your house, whether or not you want to sell it, an excellent and very cheap investment is a little book, costing 52½p, by F. Bradbury and entitled *Guide to Marks of Origin of British and Irish Silver Plate*. You can get it from most jewellers and from antique shops which specialize in silver. Using this book, with a little practice you can decide upon the date and provenance of any piece of silver without difficulty. The only other help you may need is a magnifying glass. Even people with really good eyes need this, for the marks have often been rubbed (particularly in the case of older pieces) and the details are sometimes a little difficult to make out.

**Imitations**   Anything as valuable as silver is bound to have been copied. Actual forgeries (that is, the stamping of non-silver pieces with false hall-marks) are almost unknown because of the very severe legal penalties for tampering with or forging the assay marks. But there are hundreds, if not thousands, of people who have been very disappointed to find that when they take their precious pieces to a dealer, something they have always treasured as silver is not silver at all. The two kinds of ware that are most often confused with silver are *Sheffield Plate* and electro-plated nickel silver (EPNS).

**Sheffield Plate**   This was a deliberate attempt to copy silver in somewhat cheaper materials, so that a wider public could have the benefit of 'silver' ornaments and tableware. It was made between 1740 and 1840. The material is a sort of metal sandwich, made up of thin silver, thick copper and thin silver again. There should be no difficulty in distinguishing between Sheffield Plate and real silver, because Sheffield Plate is *never hallmarked*; it would have been illegal to do so. Secondly, because of the way it was made (silver–copper–silver) many years of polishing have often worn away the outer thin layer of silver and exposed the copper beneath. This gives a quite distinct pinkish tinge on prominent parts that have suffered the most wear and polishing. Sheffield Plate was never cheap, and the workmanship was often as good as any famous silversmith could produce. It is now collected in its own right, not surprisingly—it is, after all, up to 230 years old. Some of the best products fetch extremely high prices, as high as if the material had been sterling silver.

*Typical EPNS mark copying silver hall-marks*

**EPNS**   Electro-plated nickel silver was a cheap process of plating metal with an electrically deposited film of silver. It was invented in 1840, and it was only a very short time before it had completely ousted Sheffield Plate as the everyday alternative to silver. The makers of electro-plated nickel silver items very often marked their products with a trademark or brand name that included the initials EPNS in a row of little shield-shaped die marks. These at first glance look for all the world like the hall-marks on silver. Alternatively, they stamped their initials (or symbol of the company, or anything else they liked) in similar shield-shaped marks. All this was intended to deceive the unwary public: it was perfectly legal, because the marks they used were not the official hall-marks used on silver—they just looked like them.

So beware: look first of all for the lion mark, because if it is there the piece is made of real silver. Then look for the mark of the Assay Office—the leopard's head of London, or the anchor of Birmingham, or one of the other specified and easily recognizable assay marks—and then look for the date letter.

**Cleaning silver**  More damage has been done to fine old silver by the wrong sort of cleaning than you would believe possible. If you find a piece of silver which is badly tarnished, and you want to make it look pretty before offering it for sale (or before giving it a place of honour in your house), you should clean it this way and no other:
  (a) Wash it in warm soapy water and rinse it in clean warm water.
  (b) Dry it carefully with a clean soft cloth.
  (c) Apply Goddard's Long-Term Silver Polish as directed on the bottle.
We cannot emphasize too much how important it is to clean silver with extreme care. Much of the value of really fine pieces lies in the smooth unscratched surface of the silver, and careless handling or the wrong cleaning materials can do an enormous amount of harm.

**Gold**  Gold is much rarer than silver in England. This is not only because of its much higher value, but because the English have always preferred the appearance of silver to that of gold for precious or decorative pieces. Items of gold made in England are hall-marked in accordance with much the same rules as those which apply to silver. There are special rules and special marks which apply to pieces made abroad and imported into England.

People who have gold lying about in their attic need a bank manager with a nice strong vault, rather than a book about antiques.

One particular point about gold is worth mentioning. In the course of the seventeenth and eighteenth centuries there was a strange habit of gilding silver, particularly in the case of ornate decorative pieces such as table centrepieces. This sort of large, elaborate affair is unlikely to concern us; but this gilding of silver was practised for quite a different reason on some tableware, particularly silver saltspoons. The reason is, as any housewife knows, that salt and silver disagree —after a while the spoon turns permanently black. Gold does not tarnish, and therefore quite a lot of saltspoons in silver were partially gilded ('parcel gilt' as it is often called) with a thin film of gold on both sides of the bowl of the spoon. The normal silver hall-marks are retained in cases like this.

**Brass** Sad to say there is little in the way of brass that is of interest to the antique trade or to collectors. In spite of this there is a considerable amount of apparently old brass both in antique shops and in houses. Much of it is Indian and Oriental, and stems from the days when military—and trading—families brought back large quantities of souvenirs from India and points farther east at the end of tours of duty. The evaluation of *old* Indian brassware is a highly specialized business which is beyond our scope; but let it be said now that the vast proportion of Indian brassware, including such things as huge trays, tables, gongs and elephants, is of relatively modern origin—and much of it was in fact made in Birmingham rather than in India. There was a flourishing export trade from Birmingham to Benares, the main centre of Indian brassware.

One subject which springs to mind when brass is mentioned is that of *horsebrasses*.These were originally fixed to various parts of a horse's harness as protection against the 'evil eye', but from about 1860 onwards horses were loaded with an ever-increasing number of brasses, mainly for decorative purposes. Anyone who has seen the parades of heavy horses in full regalia at agricultural shows, or at the Easter Parade in Hyde Park, will know what a magnificent sight they can be. There are very many collectors of horsebrasses. Some keep them for pure decoration to fix along old beams (particularly in public houses); some, but not many, collect them for their historical interest and value. Genuine old horsebrasses are surprisingly rare, because of the colossal number of copies which have been made. Brass of a date earlier than 1850 is a rarity in any case. Brasses that have actually been worn on a horse's harness always command much greater interest and better prices among collectors, and the same rule applies to

*Horse brass*

brasses actually attached to harness. You can usually tell if a brass has been worn on a harness, because it will show wear at two particular points, (a) at the very bottom of the disc, where it has swung with the horse's movements against the leather harness; and (b) at the top of the hanging loop, where the thin leather strap which attached it to the main harness passed through; the same movement of the horse caused friction and wear between them.

As a rule, genuine old brasses are identifiable by this wear; by their weight (old ones were much heavier than modern ones); and by the designs. Until about 1840 horsebrasses were almost invariably decorated with heavenly symbols such as the sun, moon or stars. Later (mid-Victorian) brasses often had devices associated with particular areas of England, devices such as the Staffordshire knot, the Cotswold woolbales or the Wiltshire dolphin.

Most desirable of all from a collector's point of view are complete sets of brasses mounted on the original harness. Such complete sets include the flyer (fixed to the horse's head above the ears, and usually consisting of a miniature brass swinging in a frame under a coloured horsehair brush); a nameplate; a nose-band plate; and possibly a set of latten bells, fixed in a frame above the collar and designed to warn other traffic of the cart's approach down a narrow lane.

**Pewter** Pewter is often much misunderstood and almost totally disregarded by non-collectors. The worst misconception is that it is dull and lead-coloured. Pewter plates and dishes were used by all reasonably well-off families until the general introduction of porcelain in the early eighteenth century; and it remained popular after that for flagons and tankards. It was kept clean by being scoured with sand and water, and this treatment gave it a bright silvery finish which is extremely attractive—particularly in conjunction with the oak that was the normal timber used for furniture in the seventeenth century. Collectors pay very high prices for good examples of plates, chargers (large plates or dishes) and, particularly, for flagons.

Neglected pewter does indeed tarnish to a very dark and dull lead colour. It is hardly surprising, since all pewter except that of the best quality contains lead. Only what is technically known as 'fine pewter' (used for the making of plates and dishes exclusively) is made up of tin and copper without any lead at all. Tankards and candlesticks were made from an alloy known as 'lay' which contained a proportion of lead, and some of the later and cheaper wares were made up almost entirely of lead. If you have a piece which you suspect may be pewter, you can make your own test as to the quality of the alloy. If you wash the piece in soap and water, removing all the dirt, and then rub it with a piece of clean white paper, the paper will be marked to a greater or

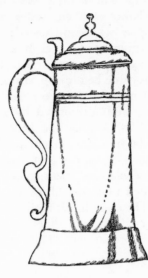

*Pewter flagon, dated about 1740*

lesser degree according to the amount of lead present in the alloy. If the paper becomes heavily marked—as if it had been rubbed with a soft lead pencil—then the pewter is of low grade and of probably late date.

Pewter tankards can be worth small fortunes in themselves. The earliest ones date from about 1600, and in the course of the next two hundred years they followed fairly well-defined changes in shape. Good pewter tankards always have lids, hinged at the handle end.

Condition is rather less important in the case of pewter than it is for almost all other forms of antiques. This is simply because objects made in pewter were nearly always meant to be used in the normal hurly-burly of domestic life, and it is therefore almost unheard-of for a pewter dish or tankard to have survived without suffering a few knocks, dents and scratches. The method of cleaning was a pretty rough-and-ready one too, and had the same result.

**Copper** The only items of copper that we shall mention are both to do with heating—warming-pans and footwarmers. Many people will be disappointed to know that the warming-pan that hangs on their wall is almost certainly a fake or a copy. Copper warming-pans were not made in this country until the beginning of the eighteenth century, but in spite of this one sees many copper ones labelled 'Elizabethan'. Brass warming-pans came before copper ones, and before the familiar shape of a round pan on the end of a long handle they were handleless and surrounded by a wooden cage to keep the hot metal away from the bedclothes.

What appear to be miniature examples of brass warming-pans are more likely to be chestnut roasters. These most useful pieces of household equipment consist of a shallow iron pan with a perforated brass lid, all on the end of a handle about 2 feet long. These are much more likely to be genuine.

The other copper (and sometimes brass also) warming device was the foot-warmer. This was designed for

*Copper railway-carriage footwarmer*

travellers, and was first used in the days of stage coaches. A copper container, usually boat-shaped and about 2 feet long, could be filled with hot water and slipped into a carpet cover to keep the traveller's cold feet warm on the long journey. They continued to be used in Victorian times for railway travellers, and in fact the railway companies produced them for hire. You could collect your empty foot-warmer, have it filled at the engine of your own train and retire in triumph to your carriage. They must have been particularly comforting for lady travellers, whose long skirts made a sort of insulated tent over the foot warmer.

**Cast iron** This may sound an unlikely material to include in what is really a treasure hunt, but the fact remains that some Victorian, and earlier, cast iron is of great interest to collectors. Of particular importance are *firebacks,* now becoming very rare. These slabs of cast iron, often 3 feet square or more, protected the back of the large open fireplaces of Elizabethan and later times and also helped to reflect the heat of the fire outwards rather than up the gaping chimney. The earliest ones are particularly interesting,

*Early sixteenth-century cast-iron fireback*

because the opportunity was taken in the casting to include simple decorations. They were cast in a sand mould, and into the sand would be pressed such utilitarian objects as a pair of scissors or a length of rope for a border; these were faithfully reproduced when the molten iron was poured in. Cast-iron firebacks are also quite often dated by the same method. Later (Georgian) examples are much more sophisticated, and the decorations often show all the classical influence which was popular towards the end of the eighteenth century.

*Pub tables*  Very much later—in fact dating from the early years of the present century—are the cast-iron tables that were made primarily for public houses. These are three-legged, about 2 feet across, circular and ornately cast. Their particular merit is that they have faces cast into the decorations at the top of each of the three legs; the most common combination is Edward VII and Queen Alexandra, but there are other models. One in particular which cricket collectors search for with great enthusiasm has the head of W. G. Grace.

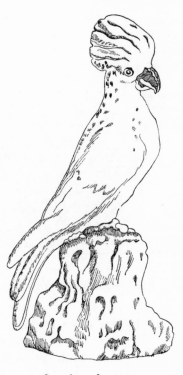

*Cast-iron door stop*

*Door porters*  These pieces of (usually) cast iron, always decorative and often very well painted, have gone completely out of fashion. They were used for holding doors open and no Victorian house was complete without several of them.

Thousands must have been produced, and one wonders where they have all gone. They were cast in various shapes, some of which became particularly popular. Among them are swans, cockatoos, lions and sheep as well as well-known personalities such as Nelson and the Duke of Wellington. Some were black-leaded, others painted. Nice examples and unusual designs are much sought-after.

*Victorian umbrella stand*

**Umbrella stands** Another Victorian and Edwardian use for cast iron was the making of decorative umbrella and walking-stick stands. They have become very popular again; interior decorators have rescued many examples in the last stages of rust to be cleaned up and restored to something like their original state. The example illustrated has a dog theme, but there are hundreds of variations, limited only by the caster's imagination —gardening, cricket, fishing, hunting—as well as thousands of plainer patterns.

I

**Scientific instruments**  This section can only scratch the surface of what is a large subject with many branches. Owners should however be aware that there is a considerable (and growing) demand for such things as early microscopes and telescopes, photographic equipment such as the magnificent mahogany and brass plate cameras of the late Victorian era (but not including box Brownies). Nineteenth-century and earlier medical equipment is wanted by specialist collectors, who search particularly for travelling medicine cabinets used by the apothecaries and early doctors, and such particular items as the short, rigid stethoscopes (which preceded the flexible model with rubber tubes), pottery leech jars and cupping glasses.

**Clocks**  The main value of a clock lies in who made it. Grandfather clocks (or long-case clocks as they are more correctly known) by 'unknown' makers are of little value as a rule; some years ago there was a thriving trade exporting old grandfather clocks to Europe by the *shipload*; the poor prices that the owners of the individual clocks received can be imagined. If, however, you have a long-case clock (or any other sort of clock for that matter) which has one of the following names engraved on the dial, the value will be in thousands of pounds rather than in hundreds—Fromanteel, Daniel Quare, Thomas Tompion, William Clement, Joseph Knibb. These were all English clock-makers of the late seventeenth century, which is regarded as the best period of clock-making. Most grandfather clocks are of Victorian date and country make. As a guide to date, clocks with brass dials were probably made before 1760; after this, white enamel or silvered dials were introduced. Another help in dating early clocks is that, before about 1680, only one hand was fitted because time-keeping was so inaccurate that it was not worth while having a minute hand as well. It was after this date too, and for the same reason, that a second ring of divisions was engraved round the dial, outside the numbers, to show the minutes. Finally, until about 1710 the dial and its surrounding hood was almost square, or at least rectangular. After that it began to be common for the top of the dial and its hood to be domed, and for a picture (sometimes moving with the clock mechanism) of the sun or the moon to be inserted in the domed space.

*Bracket clock by Thomas Tompion*

**Guns** We shall concern ourselves only with the sporting guns in this section—old military weapons (including swords and duelling pistols) form a separate subject with many expert devotees and a large bibliography of reference works.

English sporting guns are the most highly regarded in the world, and there are many people today who are shooting with guns made up to seventy years ago. A double-barrelled shotgun of conventional size (that is 12, 14 or 16 bore) in good condition is a readily saleable item. In all but the most exceptional cases, such guns would be bought to be used again, and condition is therefore important.

Pairs of guns by such makers as Boss, or Holland and Holland, can be worth more than a thousand pounds if they are in absolutely perfect condition. They should be taken to a first-class gunmaker—such as Holland and Holland themselves—for a valuation. Above all, any sporting gun of whatever age should be checked over by a gunmaker before being used. This is vitally important, and can prevent somebody from having his hand or half his face blown off. If a gun is given away, it should be given on the condition that it is examined in this way before use. It should also be mentioned that the owner of a shotgun is now required to have a certificate issued by the police and costing £1.

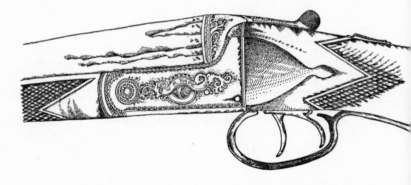

*Engraving on sporting gun*

## I I

# Old Uncle Tom Cobbleigh
# and all

We have tried in the preceding chapters to group together
into families a whole lot of things which you might find in
your attic or elsewhere in the house. This is bound to leave
a lot of other things which cannot conveniently be classified.
We shall therefore have to have a quick round-up of one or
two of the more likely objects that have been left out.

**Furniture**   There are several dozen good books on furniture,
some of them general, some of them on particular aspects;
one of them will tell you all about the better sorts of
furniture. The only pieces of furniture which you are likely
to find in your attic are the ones which you, or somebody
before you, have not known what to do with. For example,
a *shaving stand*. This Georgian and Victorian necessity has
completely gone out of fashion and use, and many people
would not recognize one for what it is. The usual model is
a round pillar of mahogany (or some cheaper wood stained
to look like it) standing on short tripod legs at the bottom,
and with a circular double-lidded box at the top, surmounted
by a tilting round mirror. The whole thing stands about 5 feet
tall, but one of the unexpected features is that the central
pillar usually contains lead counterweights which allow the
mirror to be pushed up or down by one finger. The circular
box was meant to contain razors, strops and anything else
you wanted to put in there.

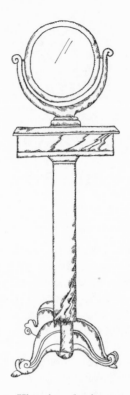

*Late Victorian shaving stand*

*Whatnots* have never found another name, for some strange reason. They are basically Victorian pieces of furniture (though they had their expensive Regency ancestors), usually in the form of three or four shelves which stand freely on the floor. They were carved and ornamented in a variety of ways, and the result is usually heavy and out of keeping with modern (or pre-Victorian) styles of furnishing. None the less they are now collected simply because they are part of the vast area known as Victoriana, and the more ornate and oppressive they are, the more popular they will be to some collector.

Many of these same remarks apply equally to some of the furniture produced in the period immediately after the First

*Rosewood whatnot*

World War. Between 1920 and 1930, there was a particular craze for bamboo or mock-bamboo furniture, especially for bedrooms. This has the great merit to collectors of being almost unique to its period, and it is therefore in some demand.

*Display cabinets* More and more people are forming collections, and as a result more and more storage and display furniture is required. Especially popular are the attractive little display tables, which consist basically of a glass-topped and glass-sided box on three or four legs. A layer of coloured velvet in one of these tables provides the best possible way of showing off one's small and treasured pieces. However, the net is now cast much wider, and collectors are snapping up even such unexpected things as shop display fittings.

**Fire equipment** We know one house where there still exists, in full working order, an old hand-pumped fire engine which must date from nearly two hundred years ago. It was horse-drawn, but when a flow of water was required it needed four to six men on each side of the engine to pump a long handle up and down; it must have been hard work.

Most of the other examples we have seen are in museums, and the opportunity of acquiring one must be rare indeed.

But there is fire-fighting equipment which is much less elaborate than this, and which is still of interest to collectors. Particularly wanted are the leather firebuckets which used to hang in every large house, often painted with the crest of the owner or merely the name of the house.

Early models of chemical fire extinguishers are *not,* as yet, collectors' items. In fact, an alarming number of houses are relying at this moment on fire-fighting equipment which was installed perhaps forty years ago. One hopes that they will never need to use it in earnest, because most of it will not work.

*Leather firebucket painted with coat of arms of Scudamore family*

**Old collections** People sometimes have the idea that collecting is almost entirely a modern hobby. This is, of course, quite untrue. All our great museums have, as a central part of their display, collections that were made during the nineteenth century. And, of course, there were famous collectors before that—Elias Ashmole and Sir John Soane being two whose collections founded complete museums. Coming closer to the attic-treasure-hunter's field, a tremendous number of collections of natural materials—particularly birds' eggs,

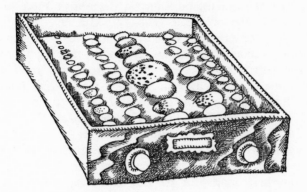

*A drawer from a birds'-egg cabinet*

*Glass dome covering 'flowers' made from seashells*

moths and butterflies—were made by our grandfathers, and by *their* fathers. These collections may be interesting in themselves to specialist museums (a descriptive letter to the director of the Natural History Museum in South Kensington, for example, would establish whether a comprehensive collection of butterflies and moths might be important) and this should be your first concern. It would be a social crime to throw away a lifetime's work without taking the trouble to find out whether it could be used by someone else. But of more interest to the general collector are the cabinets that these collections were often housed in—rows and rows of tiny drawers in extremely well-carpentered cases, sometimes with folding glass fronts. These are ideal for modern collectors, particularly for keeping such things as stamps or illustrated writing paper—in fact for anything to do with paper.

**Glass domes** No Victorian home was complete without a stuffed bird, or an arrangement of seashells, or a bunch of wax fruit and flowers, under a glass dome. A vast number of these have disappeared for ever, thrown out in horror by unsympathetic descendants. As a result, those which survive are collectors' pieces, typifying as they do the Victorian era with all its majestic decorative hotch-potch.

**Bird cages** Attractive cages, either for small birds or for parrots, are much in demand. This applies particularly to the very substantial brass cages for birds, more especially if all the fittings are still present.

# 12

# A last word

So there we are. Sort through the attic—perhaps right through the house from roof to cellar—and what will you find? Perhaps some of the things we have mentioned; almost certainly a great many that we haven't.

Every house is different, stamped with the personality of its occupants. Some people can't bear to have things out where they gather dust. Others love to be surrounded by all their most precious possessions, to remind them of earlier days and happy occasions. Some people never throw anything away: others have a complete turnout of their houses at least once a year and burn everything that has lost its usefulness. Some people live entirely in the present: others almost completely in the past.

All these differences in people's personalities will be reflected in what they have in the way of attic treasures, and where such treasures might be found. But (as we have already said once in the course of this book) don't expect to make your fortune from the contents of your attic. And don't be in too much of a hurry to dispose of them, for time is on your side: if something is valuable now, it will almost certainly be more valuable in a few years' time.

# Index

142